# SAILING

# BIG

# ON A SMALL SAILBOAT

## THIRD EDITION

## JERRY CARDWELL

### Revised and Edited by Dieter Loibner

SHERIDAN HOUSE

Third edition published 2007
by Sheridan House Inc.
145 Palisade Street
Dobbs Ferry, NY 10522
www.sheridanhouse.com

First edition 1993
Second edition 1997
Third edition 2007

*Library of Congress Cataloging-in-Publication Data*

Cardwell, J. D. (Jerry Delmas)
      Sailing big on a small sailboat / Jerry Cardwell ; revised and edited by Dieter
Loibner. — 3rd ed.
          p. cm.
      Includes bibliographical references and index.
      ISBN 978-1-57409-247-9 (pbk. : alk. paper)
      1. Sailing. 2. Sailboats. I. Loibner, Dieter, 1961- II. Title.

  GV811.6.C36 2007
  797.124-dc22                                                      2007000849

Editor: Janine Simon
Designer: Jeremiah B. Lighter


Printed in the United States of America

ISBN 13:1-57409-247-9
ISBN10:1-57409-247-2

# *Contents*

# Introduction by the Editor

It was a long and winding road that led me to editing this book about trailerable sailboats. It started, to the best of my knowledge, late in the summer of 1965 when I was about to start kindergarten in a small town in the south of Austria. My parents took it upon themselves to take me on an epic road trip to pick up my father's first "real" sailboat, a Shark catamaran in England. Long before Europe became what it is today, traveling from rural Austria to London was a journey to the far side of the world. Compared to now there was only a patchwork of highways in place. Traversing all of Western Europe also meant showing our passport, getting searched by customs at each border crossing and worrying about sufficient funds in the currencies of the respective countries to pay our way. I also remember vividly getting tossed about on our way across the stormy Channel in the bowels of a ferry from the Belgian port of Oostende to Dover, or fixing the family car—a Fiat no less—that always seemed to break down when we could least afford it.

On the way home the Fiat did OK, but somewhere on a German highway one of the trailer wheels quit. It wasn't the first such calamity, however this time it was serious. Flames engulfing the wheel made it clear that the problem wasn't just a common flat, but that one of the bearings was gone. Oh, the hassle. None of the tools fit, because all our repair kit was metric and the trailer was English, which meant that all parts had to be manufactured to imperial measurements.

Later, we always towed the boat to Croatia to sail to the then unspoiled and wonderfully desolate Kornati Islands. Anywhere we wanted to go, the boat followed us. Well, almost anywhere. I remember one trip that was highlighted by a special trailer trauma. Dad was getting a bit antsy following a vegetable truck that did 35 mph on a bumpy, curvy country road somewhere in northern Yugoslavia, today's Slovenia. At the first reasonable opportunity to pass that smoke-belching monster, the old man floored it. We made it fine, he merged back into our lane, but the boat did not. It had jumped the hitch and merrily kept on going, heading straight for the oncoming traffic. To this day, I don't know how or why the boat did not get smashed. The trailer made a gentle left turn and plowed into a grassy field, tongue and coupler first. The only damage was a broken cable for the trailer lights. Whew.

As I started to sail dinghies competitively, the trailer became a fixture in my boating life. Sweden, France, Denmark, the Netherlands, Spain, Hungary, Italy were all conquered. The adventures were fun for the most part and made memories for life: My mates and I once were detained by Italian carabinieri in Verona for not having the right contraption attached to the butt of a mast that extended one foot beyond the stern of the boat. We had a red flag, they insisted on a diagonally white-and-orange striped square with a reflector in each corner. Another time we sat around for three days in the pretty town of Porto Santo Stefano with a busted bearing, waiting for the replacement to be shipped. On an excursion to the Riviera, we entered a tunnel, trying to thread our way through rush hour in Nice. In our haste we neglected the warning signs indicating that there might not be enough clearance for our rig. We only managed by having one of the guys hang on the mast to bend the tip downward, so it wouldn't scrape on the tunnel's ceiling.

I lived and learned as my love affair with trailer boats deepened and I became more appreciative of the freedom that came with taking my vessel on a road trip. It didn't matter if I went just over the hill to the next glassy lake or to the outer reaches of the continent. Hitching up meant going places.

When the chance arose to edit the late Jerry Cardwell's book *Sailing Big on a Small Sailboat*, it was more than an assignment. It was a chance to relive those memories and connect with my humble sailing roots. Sure, much has changed since the mid-1960s, equipment has become more sophisticated and boats have become faster and more comfortable, while cars have grown bigger and gasoline has become more expensive. But one thing hasn't changed: The romance of being on the road.

So here is the third edition of this book, one that is significantly expanded and broadened to reflect the status of sailing big on small boats at the beginning of the 21st century. But my objective was to follow in the footsteps of an intrepid fellow trailerboater and do my best to keep the advice in his spirit that is defined succinctly in Cardwell's First Law of Sailing Big. It is my sincere hope that this book can impart some valuable knowledge to trailer sailors who already were bitten by the bug and maybe whet the appetite of those who are intrigued by the possibilities of one of the most versatile, fun and affordable ways to take to the water.

Dieter Loibner

# *Preface*

I do not believe that anything can compare to a warm evening on a sailboat. Sitting in the cockpit after a spring thunderstorm, watching a reluctant sun splash its orange hues on a darkening blue sky, listening to the sounds of the waves, and gazing up at the emerging stars while the moon softly announces that the world indeed continues to be whole, one acquires a sense of personal security and peace that cannot be found anywhere else.

I presume that a fair number of sailors began as I did, looking in the pages of sailing magazines and imagining the peaceful feeling of sailing and the tranquility of a night at anchor with gentle breezes, a sky filled with stars and moonlight, and a good book. I would drop anchor in a quiet cove, stretch out in the cockpit with a cool drink, and commune with nature while awaiting evenfall and time for bed in my cozy and secure cabin.

I think that thousands of people are having similar dreams, but unfortunately, the popular mythology surrounding sailing and sailors has led most of them to believe that they can't afford such a luxury. That's a pity, because if done right, sailing big on a small sailboat is within the reach of average folks even if they might think it isn't. Correcting this misconception is one of the missions of the third edition of this book and providing hands-on advice for those who dare to make their dreams come true.

One way of living such a sailing dream is to buy a small vessel and "keep it simple." That might be fine if roughing it in limited quarters is not a deterrent. In tiny boats headroom in the cabin is an illusion, so your chin seemingly is always on your knees and using the head is a major production. This is what I call "sailing small on a small sailboat." For me, cramped quarters and the associated discomfort is not part of the dream.

Although my personal preference for trailerable sailboats is in the 22- to 26-foot range, it must be noted that modern design and construction have increased space and performance on some smaller boats, a development that will be reflected in the review of boats. Still, it isn't necessary to buy more sailboat than one can possibly afford. With few exceptions, most boats included in this book have a price tag of less than $30,000 (2006) and that includes sails and trailers. So why get a new 30- or 45-footer that costs $120,000 to $350,000 or more to buy and equip?

This leads me to Cardwell's First Law of Sailing Big, the premise for the book you are holding in your hands—YOU CAN SAIL BIG ON A SMALL SAILBOAT FAR MORE EASILY AND FOR MUCH LESS MONEY THAN YOU CAN SAIL SMALL ON A BIG SAILBOAT.

# 1

# *The Possibilities*

*Buying a boat, the right boat for the right per-
son, is a very tricky thing. It is like getting lovers
together in the sense that the chemistry is either
there or it is not. You have to fall in love with a
boat before you buy it, and love being in the air
does not make for clear thinking. It is a subtle
and difficult problem.*

HUGO LECKEY, Floating

## ➢ AN INTRODUCTORY CONFESSION ◄

It is necessary to begin with a confession—I am not a lifelong
sailor. I did not have a kind, gentle, and nautical father to instruct
me in the fine art of living in harmony with the sea and sailboats.
I've only been sailing for 25 years, and all of them in sailboats less
than 30 feet long. But I have sailed in a lot of places, in vastly different conditions, on boats as tiny as the Sunfish, on open-decked
daysailers, on microcruisers, compact cruisers, and 22- to 26-foot
trailerable family sailboats. I have sailed on the very cold waters
of the small Rocky Mountain lakes, on large inland lakes in the
Midwest, TVA lakes in the middle and lower South, and in southern coastal waters. I have never chucked everything and sailed off
to Bora Bora, to Bermuda, the Virgin Islands, or the Bahamas.

I have daysailed a whole lot, and I have overnighted with my
wife and two sons on my 19-foot O'Day Mariner on a night when
the water in the bilge froze to a solid block of ice. I have spent
more weekends with my two sons on my Catalina 22 than I can remember, and I have undertaken several seven-day cruises along
the Alabama and Florida coasts on my trailerable sailboats. It has

not all been picture perfect; in fact, some sails were downright challenging, even miserable. But all of them were worth it. Each outing, no matter how long or short, had two essential highlights. One, of course, was the joy of being on the water as part of the relationship between a sailboat and the elements. The second was learning about some new gear on other boats that contributes significantly to the comfort and the enjoyment of the sport. Every time I go, I come back with new ideas and things for my trailerable sailboat that will make my next outing even better and more enjoyable. And that's what I want to share with you in this book.

## ➤ THE VENUE ◄

Over the past 20 years I have tried to read every book I could find that was remotely connected with trailerable sailboats. Each of them has proven to be less than satisfactory in one way or another, primarily because they were written with the assumption that the readers were either offshore sailors or people who could only afford to daysail or overnight by camping out on the water. That is why I wrote *Sailing Big on a Small Sailboat*. I will not refrain from using sailing terms, although I make no claim to being an old salt in this regard. My goal is to inform the reader about the possibilities of sailing like the big boys do, but in the context of smaller boats and on less challenging bodies of water, such as lakes and littoral areas. Permit me to relate a brief example to you.

Picture a quiet little marina just off the Intracoastal Waterway on the coast of Alabama. Three Catalina 22s are about to leave their slips, motor out into a small inlet, and then into the mouth of a fairly large bay, which connects with the Intracoastal Waterway. Two of the Catalina boats are well equipped, with bow pulpits and sternrails, thick cushions in the cockpit, color-coded halyards and sheets, lifelines, VHF radios, sail-control lines leading to the cockpit, and biminis to shield the occupants from the sun on this 90-degree day. The third boat has none of these things, save a bow pulpit.

The three vessels motor out, and after a brief conversation on their VHF radios, boats one and two agree to point into the wind and hoist their sails. At the skipper's request, the crew remains seated in the cockpit while grabbing the main and jib halyards to hoist both sails. The boats bear off, everybody opens a cold beverage, and they are under way. On boat three, the skipper also heads into the wind but has to ask his crew to go forward to raise the sails. The crew leaves the cockpit, climbs onto the cabintop to get to the base of the mast, grabs a halyard and begins to pull. However, because all the halyards are exactly of the same color and diameter, he raises the jib instead of the mainsail and all of a sudden mayhem: The jib sheet is cleated, which causes the sail to fill, and the boat's bow to fall off the wind. The boat starts to heel and the crew automatically grabs the mast to steady himself. It is only after the skipper has managed to regain control and head the boat back up into the wind that he identifies the main halyard correctly and raises the sail. After cleating it he scrambles back into the sun-drenched cockpit. Like on the other boats, skipper and crew open a cool drink, but what a struggle they had to get to this point. And now, because the boat doesn't have a sternrail or lifelines to lean back on, they have to sit bolt upright as they too get under way.

After four hours of sailing under the burning sun, our intrepid sailors on boat three will return with tired backs and exposed skin that can best be described as "medium-rare." This is an example for the difference between sailing "big" and sailing "small" on a small sailboat.

## ➢ THE RATIONALE ➤

People are attracted to the wonders, the mystery, the challenge, and the pure joy of sailing. Some like the competition of racing, while others seem to welcome the opportunity for endless tinkering with their boats, even if they seldom actually sail them. Still others own boats simply to enjoy time on the water. Because sailing can be so many different things to so many different people, the boats they are choosing are not the same.

Maybe it's the cycle of economic prosperity and uncertainty that favors one style of sailing or another. Perhaps it has something to do with the aging population of baby boomers who have grown wiser, more practical, and more interested in real substance rather than frills, but many still consider pocket cruisers a great way to enjoy the pleasure of sailing without breaking the bank. Despite repeated predictions of the demise of the category, the market for trailerable sailboats with cruising capabilities remains strong, especially in inland areas and with novices to the sport. But that's not the end of it. Many people who are tired of the complexity, equipment and maintenance costs, crew requirements, and limited sailing time on their big boats are downsizing in order to continue sailing and do more of it. Smaller boats are not only fun, they are far less complicated and can be sailed comfortably alone or with a small crew. The simplicity and usability of these craft exemplifies the less-is-more thinking that can make life easier, cheaper, much more enjoyable.

When I bought a used Catalina 22, almost all of my friends and coworkers made comments like "what did you do, rob a bank?" or they would laugh and call me a "social climber." The fact that sailing small is a reasonably inexpensive leisure activity seems to be lost on too many. Sailing's long-standing reputation as a sport for the wealthy is a product of the days before fiberglass, when boats were not mass-produced and their acquisition was out of reach for earners of an average income. Media hype and the great expenses of high-profile sailing events such as the America's Cup, the Volvo Ocean Race and the Grand Prix racing circuit also depict sailing as a pastime for the elite, thus deterring many people from trying it.

In recognition of this misunderstanding, Robert Hobbs, a former president of the United States Sailing Association, once sent a letter to the sailing media requesting the following: "In an effort to increase the appeal of the sport of sailing to the general public and in an attempt to dispel the elitist image often associated with our sport, I would appreciate it if you would refer to 'sailing' instead of 'yachting'." Interestingly, I once had a status-conscious colleague who often spoke of yachting at his summer home, conjuring images in my mind of a big cruising boat. Later, I was amused when I learned that during the summer he did his "yachting" on a little 14-foot West Wight Potter. Of course, like other activities such as golf, hunting, fishing, auto racing, and powerboating, sailing certainly can become quite expensive, but I'm here to tell you that it doesn't have to be.

If you are like me and don't have a limitless supply of money but still dream of going sailing, I want to make the case for trailerable sailboats that allow you to live your dream while participating in one of the few remaining leisure activities that can present a challenge, provide freedom, adventure, companionship, and solitude at the same time.

### ➢ GOOD REASONS FOR BUYING SMALL ≺

Gerry Hutchins of the Hutchins Company in Clearwater, Florida, the firm behind Com-Pac Yachts, is an optimist by trade even in times when the economy is sputtering. When asked about the prospects of the small-boat market, he said, "We feel the time is ripe for a shift toward smaller boats. As access to the water becomes more costly and less convenient in some areas, customers will re-evaluate where and how they spend their money." As the manufacturer of boats between 14 and 35 feet and a builder that produces only about 120 vessels per year, Hutchinson is a niche player. Several of the Com-Pac yachts along with many other domestically-built pocket cruisers show that $30,000 for a new boat with trailer and sails is not a fantasy budget. Better still, it's often enough for a few options that go towards sailing big. Just in case someone suggests that 20 to 26 feet is "awfully small" for cruising, the correct answer is that size matters less than versatility, affordability and fun. What good is a yacht, anyway, if it lives in a marina hundreds of miles from home and gets used a couple of times every year when the alternative could be sailing every weekend and taking the show on the road when Father Frost comes knocking? Before I list my reasons for buying small, I would like to suggest three reasons for buying your trailerable sailboat new:

- Emotion: Even the most devoted buyer of used boats likes to kick the fenders of a new one and imagine what it's like to sit down with the dealer and go through the list of options, colors and gear that make a new boat a personalized dreamboat.
- Fiddling vs. sailing: Leisure time is scarce, so there must be a balance for maintaining a vessel vs. using it in the intended context. On new boats things are less likely to break, which means they won't have to be replaced or repaired and that translates into more time on the water.
- Warranty: Multi-year, transferable and non pro-rated warranties on hull structure and blistering have become more common in the industry. Several manufacturers offer extended warranties for electronics, refrigeration and key engine parts and to some shoppers that is peace of mind and reason to buy new.

### Affordability

A purchase price around or below $30,000 is within reach and makes it easier to pay cash or finance your boat. You can buy a trailerable sailboat in the 22- to 26-foot range for *a lot less* than a 30- to 40-foot sailboat. To give you an extreme example, a buyer will pay about $21,000 or approximately $800 per foot for a new MacGregor 26 including trailer and sails, while a new Bavaria 30 cruiser, an aggressively priced entry-level 31-foot cruising boat, costs upward of $110,000, or more than $3,500 per foot. And that price does not include all available options. I think a $89,000 difference between an affordable new trailerable sailboat and an "affordable" new 31-foot cruising boat is a convincing reason to go small.

Of course, the boats used in this example are not meant to be compared directly since they serve different styles of sailing, however they both are means to get people out on the water for a pleasant time. Both products come from high-volume producers, so these figures illustrate the difference in initial cost between a trailer-sailer and a traditional cruising boat quite well. It also explains why trailer boats continue to be immensely popular.

Price differences between used boats are as dramatic, if not even more so. With the advent of the Internet as a tool for market research, comparison shopping and finding great deals has become more convenient than ever. If you are willing to fix up a used boat, the dream can be yours for under $10,000. (See Chapter 8.)

### Cost of Ownership

Small boat, small worries. Little things that need fixing or replacement take a smaller bite out of the boat budget than big stuff. Small boats don't need a marina berth that goes up in cost annually or might be in danger of disappearing. Their mooring is the trailer that's parked in the backyard or in a storage lot. Dry sailing also cuts down on bottom maintenance, which is a regular, messy and costly chore.

Buying small leaves you with enough money to upgrade the smaller boat for comfortable sailing and weekend cruising, pay for routine maintenance, and perhaps even dry storage.

### Availability

Just three major U.S. manufacturers—Catalina, MacGregor, and Hunter—have combined to produce tens of thousands of trailerable sailboats in the 22- to 26-foot range over the last few decades. But there are also plenty of others who have built and continue to build capable and well-respected boats in this range. For the manufacturers it's a numbers game, but one that works out well for trailer boaters. Profit margins on small boats are slim, which favors builders who can turn out large numbers of the same model and sell them at attractive prices. Many boats on the market means that there is a variety of models to choose from, depending on individual tastes and preferences and, equally as important, that there's a large inventory of used boats competitively priced. Taking this thought one step further, owning a popular trailersailer is like owning a popular car: Replacement parts are easy to come by.

### Portability

There is a big difference between going places at 5 knots in a nasty sea or at 55 mph on the freeway. Being able to change sailing venue quickly and easily by taking the boat on a road trip is an invigorating aspect, and an escape by trailer also sounds good for getting out of the next hurricane's path.

You can put a 2000- to 3000-pound sailboat on its trailer, hitch it to your vehicle, and head out of town every weekend. Try that with a 10,000-pound, 31-foot cruiser and you will lose your transmission before you get out of the driveway. Sure, a 31-foot keelboat can go on the road, but that requires professional treatment (e.g., removing the keel and rudder from the hull), permits to haul an oversized load, a special truck and insurance and a tidy sum of your money.

If you are still unconvinced about your decision to buy a trailerable sailboat, get a map and draw a circle that equals a 150-mile diameter around where you live. Now count the number of lakes, rivers, and reservoirs inside the circle. Each one is a different venue for a weekend trip with a trailerable sailboat. You can't do that with a 31-footer!

MacGregor 26. Ready to launch! Running the motor in reverse or giving the boat a gentle push will slide it off the trailer.

### Liveability

Well designed trailerable sailboats between 22 and 26 feet (and a few of the smaller ones) offer all the amenities you need to live on board in reasonable comfort for several days or even for a couple of weeks. Your sailboat is your home on the water. On most of these trailerables there is a "kitchen," a "living room," a "bathroom," and one or two "bedrooms." Admittedly these areas are not exactly palatial, but they are defined spaces, nevertheless. Combine these areas with the standing headroom provided by a hinged cabin top (pop-top) and a cockpit tent, and a pocket cruiser can be very liveable.

### Sailability

A modern trailerable sailboat is easy to sail, with some minor modifications even by one person. It is a basic tenet of sailing that a larger boat is more complex to handle, meaning that you either need a few extra bodies or some nifty technology like power winches, or hydraulic systems that assist with sail handling. That's when sailing starts to become either cumbersome or expensive or both, which defeats the purpose. You and your spouse, your son or daughter, or a friend, should be able to operate the boat with ease, because that is part of the fun and promotes frequent use. Lack of crew should never be the reason to stay ashore. Single-handed sailing is very much part of small-boat culture, but much less so on a conventionally rigged 30- or 40-footer, and especially not for beginners.

### Raceability

If you are the competitive type and want to participate in racing, trailerable sailboats have a lot to offer. Aside from racing them with and against peers on your home waters, you can take them on the road to match up against other folks and get to know other venues in the process (see Portability, above). If you'd want to sail else-where on a bigger, non-trailerable boat, there is the problem of de-livering the craft on its own keel or by truck. Either way, you probably will have to hire professionals to do it for you. Then there is the logistic challenge of getting the sailing crew and all the gear and supplies to that venue and back.

### Cruisability

If a boat is affordable, easy to take places, simple to sail, easy to fix, and comfortable to stay on, it is more likely to be used, and used often. Of course, if you will only be fulfilled by sailing off to Bora Bora or battling your way around Cape Horn, trailersailing is not for you. If, on the other hand, you have the desire to use your own skills and abilities to get your sailboat from one place to another over a three- or four-day period, a trailerable sailboat is all you need. It can take you to new and exciting places for a few days, simply to get away or to explore. On each trip you will meet new people, discover new coves and sloughs, and learn more about your boat and yourself.

Best of all, you don't have to rough it like a backpacker in the high country. Just like on bigger boats, you can keep cool, lounge around, light up the cabin, and keep clean. You can sleep in comfort, go for a dip, curl up and read or listen to some good music. You can prepare meals that deserve that name, even barbecue in the cockpit, and enjoy a glass of wine with dinner. On the way to your destination you navigate the little ship like you would any other, using an automatic tiller pilot to keep your hands free. If you like gizmos you can have them: A VHF radio, a GPS with chartplotter, a depth sounder and speedometer. In other words, on a trailerable sailboat you can cruise in comfort and safety like on a larger vessel.

If you want your sailboat to be a status symbol, a trailerable sailboat might not fit the bill. But if going sailing is all you want and you intend to do it with ease and in acceptable comfort without worrying about year-round slip fees, costly maintenance, and huge loan payments, a trailerable sailboat may be just the ticket.

### ➤ A QUESTION OF DEFINITION ◄

If a boat is capable of being trailered behind a well-powered family car, truck, van or Sport Utility Vehicle, it is called a "small" sailboat, so the boats discussed in this book fall into this category. The notion of "small" is an interesting concept. When we were living in Bowling Green, Kentucky, we owned an old English Tudor house with a living room that was 25 feet long. One winter afternoon I stood at one end of that room and imagined a sailboat that was long enough to reach the other end of the room. I suggest you do the same. If your living room isn't that long, step off 25 feet from a tree outside to get a feel for what the distance will be from bow to stern on a 25-foot sailboat. You will agree that the distance doesn't seem "small." While 20 or 25 feet might be short on the water, a beam of 8 feet 6 inches is not considered small by the law, which requires a special permit for over-wide loads to be trailered on U.S. highways or freeways. The requirements vary slightly from state to state, but 8 feet 6 inches is the critical point almost everywhere, so the decision was made to review only boats with maximum beam equal to or less than that.

## ➤ TRAILERABLE SAILBOAT BASICS ≺

Trailerable cruising boats have come on the market en force in the 1970s, and hundreds of models have been introduced. Modern materials and composite construction technologies have made smaller boats more seaworthy and spacious inside, so we will take a look at a few of those too, although the focus will remain on boats in the 22- to 26-foot range that are currently in production. But before we discuss the boats in more detail, let's examine some of the various parts of a typical trailerable sailboat and familiarize ourselves with their nomenclature.

### Hull

The part of the boat that floats is called the *hull*. On the underside of the hull most boats have two appendages: The *keel* or *centerboard*, which provide lateral resistance so the boat can sail upwind and—in the case of the keel—ballast, so the boat doesn't capsize. At or near the stern of the hull there is the *rudder*, which is primarily used to steer the boat and also provides lateral resistance. A boat's rudder may or may not be permanently attached to the hull. As shown in Figure 1-1, some boats have fixed fin keels that extend two to four feet below the waterline, defining how much draft the boat has. Some keels may have ballast bulbs or wing shapes at the bottom, which can help improve the sailing capabilities. Some boats have keels that can be raised and lowered, or a combination of a retractable centerboard or daggerboard and internal water ballast, which gives them access to very shallow water.

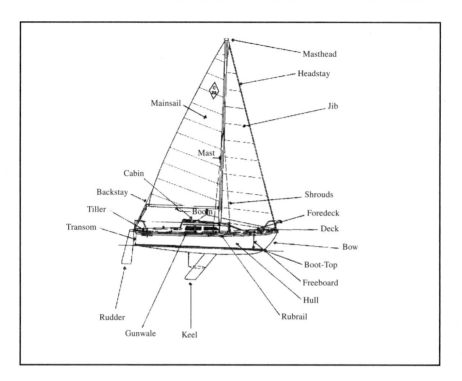

Figure 1-1. Basic parts of a trailerable sailboat

At the bottom edge of the boot-top is the boat's waterline, which defines how deep the hull is immersed in the water when floating on its designed lines. The painted or molded-in stripe that runs around the lower part of the hull above the waterline is called the *boot stripe*. The area where hull meets deck is known as the *gunwale* or the hull/deck joint. Often a *rubrail* conceals the hull/deck joint, which commonly is held together by a combination of laminate and fasteners or through-bolts. Trailerable sailboats are usually made up of four distinct fiberglass parts—the hull, the hull liner, the deck, and the deck liner. The hull and hull liner and the deck and deck liner are typically fiberglassed together to form a rigid structure, and then the hull and deck are joined at the gunwale.

The area of the hull between the waterline and the gunwale is known as the *topsides,* and the height of the topsides is called the *freeboard.* Other factors aside, the higher the freeboard, the less likely you will get hosed with spray when sailing to weather. A word of caution: too much of a good thing still will be too much. The more equipment and gear you add to the boat for sailing big, the more weight you add, which reduces the freeboard and the vessel's performance.

I have a friend who has so much stuff on his Catalina 22 that the boat sits deeper in the water than its design waterline suggests. Although he now enjoys the benefit of a slightly longer waterline, the extra weight and the increased wetted surface eradicate this desirable effect and make the boat sluggish, because the heavier boat didn't gain in sail area. It's akin to the difference of driving a car empty and fully loaded. Loading down a small boat (a term that is beautifully descriptive) doesn't help performance, alters its behavior in a seaway and affects its maneuverability. The solution is to be weight-conscious and selective about what needs to be on the boat and what can come off.

### Deck

The flat surfaces inboard of the gunwales are considered the *deck.* The area of the deck between the point of the bow and the front of the cabin trunk is called the *foredeck.* On most trailerable sailboats you will notice that the edge of the deck is raised a little, usually about an inch. That's called a *toerail,* and is a useful feature that prevents slipping off when walking on the side deck or working forward of the mast.

Immediately behind the foredeck the *coachroof* indicates the highest part of the cabin, the space down below that houses most of the boat's accommodations. Cabins come in a wide variety of configurations and layouts, which are discussed later in the book. Behind the cabin is the *cockpit,* the command center for the boat's operation that will be discussed in more detail in Chapter 3.

### Standing Rigging

Perhaps the most obvious thing about a sailboat is the *mast*, a long spar projecting straight toward the sky, used to hold up the sails. On modern trailerable sailboats the mast is made of extruded aluminum or, in rare cases, from carbon fiber, which is lighter and stronger than aluminum, but also very expensive.

As Figure 1-1 illustrates, the mast is held in place by wires called *stays* and *shrouds*, which make up the standing rigging. The shrouds attach to the chainplates on deck and the hounds approximately three quarters or more up the mast. The *headstay* is held by two attachment points: One up on the mast at the hounds (the exact position depends on the boat's rig design) and the other down at the bow, at the so-called *stemhead* fitting. If the boat has a backstay (not all do, depending on the rig design) it runs from the masthead to the stern. The head- and backstays keep the mast stable in a forward and aft direction while the shrouds keep the mast from falling over the side.

The shrouds are often held steady by rigid spreaders, which are attached to the mast high above deck. This results in more effective support angles and a stiffer spar. The stays and shrouds are made of stainless steel and can be adjusted by turnbuckles at their bottom ends, or in the case of an adjustable backstay, by a line on a strong purchase.

The boom attaches to the mast by way of a gooseneck fitting and the foot of the mainsail attaches to the boom. Modern designs often have a loose-footed mainsail that is only attached by its tack and clew. Together the mast, boom, spreaders, stays, and shrouds are simply known as the rig.

### Other Rig Equipment

Many trailerable sailboats are delivered with masthead lights for sailing at night, steaming lights, or running lights (see below). Spotlights mounted on the underside of the spreaders pointing downward help illuminate the deck. Most boaters will have a Windex or other apparent-wind direction indicator mounted at the top of the mast for a better and more efficient sail trim. Many sailors attach the antenna for their VHF radio to the mast top to increase their transmission and reception ability. In addition, if you sail on open waters or in diminished visibility, a radar reflector can be hoisted into the rig so other vessels are able to pick up the echo of your boat on their radar. All in all, the mast on a trailerable sailboat can be home to a host of devices, which contribute to safety, convenience and comfort and make it possible to sail big.

### Navigation Lights

Today, many trailerable sailboats with cruising capabilities come with navigation lights installed and ready to use, or they are prepared for the installation of an after-market product. A boat must have three running lights, which must be turned on at dusk. Two of these running lights are the port (red) and starboard (green) lights. If you are approaching a boat at night and you see a red running light ahead, you know that you are to its port side. The other skipper will see your starboard running light and know that he is on your starboard side.

A third running light is white in color and is mounted on the stern of the boat. Thus, if you are sailing at night and you see a white light coming closer, you know you are most likely overtaking another boat from behind. If you want a good practical education in keeping track of running lights on recreational and commercial vessels, spend a few nights near the shipping lanes out on Long Island Sound or any other waterway with dense traffic. Running lights are extremely important and you should make certain that they function well, are good and bright, and meet all Coast Guard requirements.

Boats in our size range must have either two separate sidelights (red/green) or one bicolor light on the bow with a range from straight forward to 112.5 degrees aft on both sides and a white stern light that ranges from straight astern to 67.5 degrees on each side. Thus, all three lights cover a full circle. Sailboats under 65 feet can substitute a tricolor light for separate side and stern lights. A boat of more than 16 feet in overall length, running under engine, is also required to have a steaming light, which must be above the sidelights and cover a range from straight ahead to 112.5 degrees on each side. At anchor outside a designated anchorage, a 360-degree white light must be displayed, usually in the mast top. The required visibility range of these lights for boats under 40 feet are 1 nautical mile for the sidelights and 2 nautical miles for all others.

If your sailing plans don't include a lot of night trips, consider removable lights that plug into a double-contact socket. If your boat isn't properly wired, there is the option of portable battery-powered LED navigation lights.

## ➢ THE SAILBOATS ◁

A trailerable sailboat is a marvel of design, engineering, and construction. Companies involved in the design, building and marketing of trailerables must address several challenges if they are to succeed in this segment of the sailboat market. First is the problem of weight. A gross vessel weight of two or three tons is not a lot for a boat with a lead keel (which can make up approximately 50 percent of the displacement) but it is a load to trailer. This means that the owner is forced to use a heavy truck or an S.U.V. with enough power to tow it. Gasoline prices and environmental concerns about global warming are a growing concern, so heavy boats that need gas-guzzlers to tow them seem more and more counterintuitive. Another issue is the ease of operation, e.g. when setting up the rig, raising the mast, launching and retrieving, and sailing singlehandedly. And last but not least, the space equation needs to be solved. How to design a compact and lightweight boat that's safe and fun to sail, and offers sufficient accommodations below for a couple to head out for an extended weekend? In many ways, that's what trailerable sailboats with cruising capabilities have achieved.

Construction techniques involving fiberglass laminate allow manufacturers to make boats strong enough to be safe and light enough to be trailerable. Just imagine how heavy a 26-foot sailboat would be if it were built from steel or wood, strong enough to withstand the pounding of wind and sea. Fiberglass laminate, when properly laid up and cured can take up to 2500 pounds of force per square inch. Another advantage of this construction method is the ability to make a large number of the same model by using industrialized manufacturing processes, laminating hull and deck from the same mold over and over again.

Of course, fiberglass has been around for 50 years and no longer represents the cutting edge of building materials, but in combination with incremental improvements in building techniques that include resin infusion, vacuum-bagging and the use of closed-foam core materials, fiberglass laminates still offer the best bang for the buck in recreational boating. Racing boats, for example, are built in smaller numbers and are often less subjected to budget constraints, so builders use lighter and stronger materials like carbon fiber for hull and rig, which produces better performance but at the same time requires much more complex construction methods. It's clear, therefore, why fiberglass still is the building material of choice for almost all of today's trailerable sailboats.

### Ballast

Every sailboat needs ballast—it is a necessary evil. If a boat remains in the water year round, a fixed keel is less of a concern than it is for a vessel that lives on a trailer and needs to go up and down steep launch ramps or mountain passes. But ballast is what makes a sailboat work. It produces righting moment that counteracts the wind's force, which not only propels the craft, but also heels it over. If a boat heels too far, it is getting knocked down. If it stays down that's called a capsize. That's not a big deal on small sailing dinghies that have live ballast (meaning the crew weight) and plenty of built-in flotation so they can be easily righted. But capsizing is certainly not on the short list of entertainment possibilities for a leisure sail on a pocket cruiser in the context of this book.

To prevent such mishaps, trailerable sailboats use lead or iron as external ballast in their keels. Alternatively, they might be equipped with a ballasted centerboard that's enclosed in fiberglass. As mentioned earlier, keels and centerboards also act as a lateral plane and keep the boat from drifting sideways when sailing to weather.

The advantage of retractable keels or centerboards is that when they are in their up-position, the boat has very little draft, which allows it to enter shallow water to float on and off a trailer at the launch ramp rather than waiting in line and/or paying money for a hoist. The downside is a loss of interior space to the mechanism that is necessary for raising or lowering a heavy appendage.

Sometimes manufacturers opt to combine a centerboard with internal ballast, which could be lead that's laminated into the bottom of the hull. But there is another option. To reduce draft and weight, the MacGregor Yacht Corporation introduced a model that uses water ballast instead of lead. The MacGregor 26 has a large tank (ca. 250 gal.) molded into the bottom of the hull, which can be flooded with seawater. When the boat is launched, a small valve is opened and the tank is gravity-filled with 1,200 pounds of water. When the tank is full, the valve is closed, and presto, there's a ballasted boat. After sailing, the vessel is floated onto the trailer, the valve is opened, and as the boat is pulled up the launch ramp the water drains, leaving a remarkably light boat that is easy to tow with a family car. But there is another reason why the MacGregor 26 uses water ballast: If the tanks are empty and the boat is equipped with a strong outboard motor, it turns into a powerboat that is capable of towing a water skier, so it serves a function that is not typical for a sailboat.

While the benefits are easy to understand and make the boat appealing to non-sailors, it is necessary to explain that water ballast is less efficient in producing righting moment when the boat sails to weather and heels to the wind. The specific weight of water is much less than that of lead or cast iron so you need much more of it. This is compounded by the fact that it is stored near the level of the boat's waterline instead of three or four feet farther below in a keel fin and/or bulb. Therefore, the center of gravity of water-ballasted boats tends to be higher, which reduces the righting moment. As a result, these boats are not as "stiff" when sailing to weather, meaning they heel sooner and farther than they would with a lead keel and a higher center of gravity also can produce an uncomfortable motion in a seaway. Manufacturers of trailerable boats with water ballast have listened to their customers and addressed these issues in their newer models, e.g. the Mac-Gregor 26M now has additional 300 pounds of internal lead ballast in the bottom of the hull.

Water ballast can enhance sailing performance as an additional source of righting moment in conjunction with a lead keel like it is seen on racing yachts, but it is a complex solution. For maximum efficiency it is carried in tanks that are built into the sides of the hull rather than the bottom. Only the tanks on the windward side of the boat are filled, and when the boat tacks the water has to be released or pumped across to the other side.

A brief mention of canting ballast should be made. The righting moment of a boat is increased by canting the keel to the windward side with the help of hydraulics and electrical power. When the system was developed in the late 1990s, it was predicted to revolutionize sailing. It has certainly increased the performance on large and expensive race boats, but it has yet to appear in production boats of less than 40 feet.

### Stepping and Unstepping the Mast

Except on the smallest of dinghies, raising and lowering the mast can be a challenge. Really tall masts need a crane, but even if they are only 25 feet high, they need extra muscle power. Sometimes this extra pair of arms is hard to come by because the task looks daunting. It can be a major bottleneck in the progression from road to water and vice versa, so builders have developed simple lever systems to assist the trailer-sailor in raising the mast. Almost all of them use some combination of block and tackle in conjunction with the existing winches on the sailboat. MacGregor claims that a young child is strong enough to raise the mast when assisted by the company's optional mast-raising solution. ComPac Yachts offers a similar system, called the Mastendr rigging system. It uses the boom vang tackle and a temporary steel strut to produce the leverage one person needs to raise and lower the hinged mast by him/herself. The wires of the standing rigging are pre-tensioned and are tightened with quick-tensioning levers. Catalina's system uses the winch post on the trailer to accomplish the same.

## ➤ BOAT CHOICES ≺

There are literally hundreds of trailerable boats that were and still are being produced. Just visit one of the more broadly used broker or used-boat Web sites and define some very general search parameters such as "sail," "20 to 26 feet" and "fiberglass." Nothing else. On www.boats.com such a query will yield hundreds, even thousands of individual boats from many different manufacturers, some of them small and exotic, some of them large and ubiquitous. To keep the flood of available trailerable sailboats from overwhelming this book, some decisions had to be made to define the selection of boats. None of them are hard and fast, but taken as a framework they characterize the sample rather succinctly:

- Weight: At a time when the adverse effects of global warming and their sources are slowly being recognized, we like to recommend boats that can be towed by a small truck/van or a family sedan/station wagon, therefore the weight of most listed boats does not exceed 4,000 pounds by much.
- Length: Almost any boat is trailerable. It all depends on how much effort and money is necessary to get it on the road and back into the water. For daysailing, weekending or family cruising, it is imperative to be able to singlehand the boat on the launch ramp and under sail, or sail it with one other adult and perhaps one or two small kids. On the other hand, basic comfort is important, which points to boats that are no less than 22 feet of overall length.
- Beam: Above 8 feet 6 inches the width of any trailerable boat becomes an issue and requires permits, therefore the listed boats do not exceed this beam. The good news is that smaller boats are both lighter and narrower so the weight and permit issues doesn't affect them. For more information about trailer issues, see Chapter 9.
- Price: Although the dollar amount in your pocket has much to do with what kind of boat you will end up with, it should not be the primary criterion when you start researching different products. In the day of the Internet, it is always possible to find a boat that fits your budget, but first determine what kind of boat fits your style of sailing and personal preferences. Some of the reviewed models have been on the market for a long time, so there is a large inventory of used boats available, with some listed for less than $4,500, depending on age and condition. On the high end a seaworthy new trailerable pocket cruiser from Europe might go for $65,000 or more. The prices listed with the specifications are approximate (for 2007) and include the basic new boat, one set of sails (main and jib) and a trailer. They do not include options or destination charges.

Catalina 22 MKII. A thorough makeover of this Hall-of-Fame pocket cruiser
created more beam, more space and more comfort below.

- Models: Only boats that were in production in 2006 were
  selected. Some of them are new, some of them are updated
  classics but all of them have distinctive character. Also included is one manufacturer from Europe who established a
  reputation for exploring new approaches to design that's
  not necessarily inspired by traditional thinking. While this
  might not be reflecting the mainstream's taste, it provides
  a different and perhaps refreshing perspective.

### Catalina

Catalina offers three 22-footers, which all serve different aspects of the small-boat sailing market. The Ur-Catalina 22, which has been around since the mid-seventies has morphed into the updated **Catalina 22mkII** and the **Catalina 22 Sport**, while the **Capri 22** is a new rendition of a popular design that came later. All three can't deny their heritage, despite upgrades and modernizations.

To be around for as long as the Catalina 22, a design has to be seaworthy and practical for a variety of purposes, from family cruising to hard-core racing. Three decades and thousands of boats after its inception, there was plenty of user feedback for Catalina to incorporate in a facelift. What do users want most? More space. Compared to the original Catalina 22, the cabin of the successor is nearly 10 inches wider, which is a world on boats of this size.

With some creativity four adults can fit, at least for a night or two, with two in the saloon and two in the V-berth. The interior is open and airy, which is good for ventilation, but provides very little privacy. The chemical toilet is not enclosed and lives forward of the port bulkhead, under the V-berth's center cushion. Only an optional curtain can close off this area to provide modest privacy. Toilets under a bunk are nobody's favorite for many practical and olfactory reasons, but on small boats that's often the only practical solution.

The saloon table is fixed and has cup holders built in. It is mounted immediately aft of the V-berth area, which could make it difficult for larger persons to find enough legroom. An optional galley with sink, stove, cutting board and storage slides out from under the cockpit, but when stowed, it might pinch the legroom on the starboard saloon berth.

The ice chest, strategically positioned, doubles as a companionway step. Under the settees there are molded fiberglass-lined stowage compartments that are handy for letting supplies and stuff disappear. A pivoting hatch for the pop-top extends the headroom, so

Catalina 22 Sport. Dimensions and weight are very similar to those of the original model.

an adult can stand up and stretch. The additional beam also extended the deck space, which provides enough room and good footing for walking forward. The absence of teak in grabrails and cockpit coamings produces a utilitarian look, but simplifies maintenance.

The cockpit with its traditional, closed stern is large enough for a family of four to sail safely and lounge comfortably. The port locker holds a portable gas tank for the outboard motor, while the starboard locker stores larger items. Drain holes through the transom above the waterline make the cockpit self-bailing.

The boat is offered with three different keel versions, including a retractable (swing) keel, and two fixed keels, one with a standard fin, the other with a wing profile and shallow draft. Interestingly, Catalina's specifications show that the short keel has less ballast than the deeper standard keel. If your plans include frequent road trips with the boat, you may want to consider the standard swing keel. If you are tickled by shallow water venues, the wing keel might be the way to go.

The deck-stepped masthead rig with fore- and backstay and two pairs of shrouds is simple and versatile and can accommodate various sizes of headsails and an optional symmetrical spinnaker. To raise and lower the mast singlehandedly, Catalina offers the option of a telescoping pole with a tackle that's mounted on the trailer tongue.

Catalina also tried to keep the boat eligible for one-design racing. According to the company, on the Catalina 22mkII "all underwater surfaces, rigging and sailplan have not been changed."

Still, there was demand for a more one-design-oriented version, which is why the company introduced the Catalina 22 Sport, "a production boat that more accurately reflects the original dimensions and weight." So if you are intent on experiencing the 70s spirit and hate combing the dry-storage lots of the marinas far and wide to find that pristine vintage Catalina 22, there is an out. Catalina explains the resurrection of the original with the intention to "encourage more family racing with the thousands of first-generation 22s by offering an alternative to finding an older boat, and restoring it just to be competitive in the dozens of established Catalina 22 fleets."

There is a third 22-foot model from Catalina, the Capri 22, which company president Gerald Douglas defines as a typical day-sailer, "something that people would have near their weekend house." This model is offered with two keel versions, an enclos-able head compartment, a racing package that includes asymmet-rical spinnaker and backstay tension adjuster, a standard or a tall rig and corresponding smaller or larger sail areas. Both, the Sport and the Capri have large cockpits and amenities for daysailing or for a weekend, which makes either one of these vessels a logical step up from a dinghy to small-boat cruising.

If you like your small sailboat bigger still, and like Catalina's approach, there is the **Catalina 250**, a boat that's been around since the mid-1990s. Three feet more in overall length makes the 250 a much bigger boat than the 22-footers. Nowhere are the dif-ferences more obvious than in the cabin, which has three distinctly separated areas, the V-berth forward, the saloon with a fixed galley and the aft double berth under the cockpit.

Molded-in toerails on the foredeck, sail control lines that are led aft into the cockpit, adjustable jib leads, full-batten main with jiffy reefing, roller-furling genoa, an open transom, rail seats in

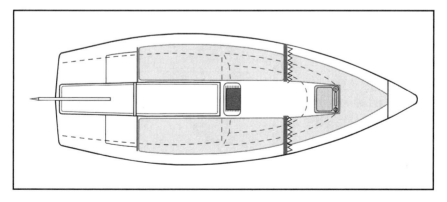

Capri 22 accommodations. Gentle curves in the cockpit make for comfortable lounging at the dock. Adding a portable head and a galley module to the interior turn this daysailer into a weekender.

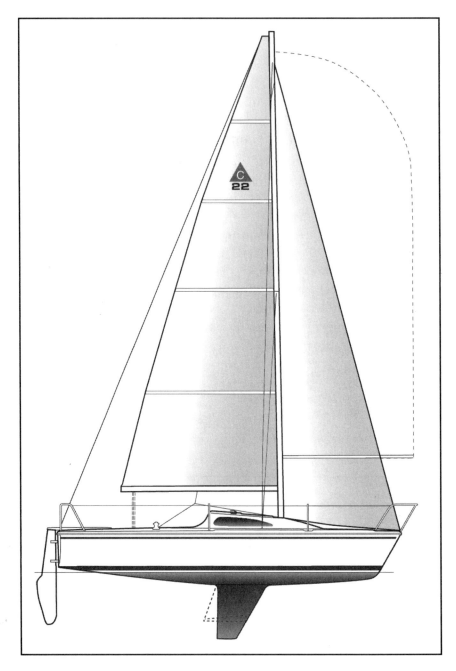

Capri 22 sail plan. The boat's one-design hull and simple rigging are the keys to sailing efficiency.

the pushpits, a removable cockpit table, enclosed head compartment with ventilation, a galley with sink, stove and manual freshwater system, the 12-volt DC electrical system and an optional inboard diesel with Saildrive transmission set the 250 apart from its smaller siblings.

The boat is offered with either a wing keel or a centerboard/water ballast combination, which makes it light on the trailer. However, mind the 8-foot-6-inch beam, for which a permit might be required.

**Catalina 22mkII**

| | |
|---|---|
| LOA | 23'10" |
| LWL | 19'4" |
| Beam | 8'4" |
| Sail Area (100% jib) | 205 sq. ft. |
| Mast height | 29'1" |
| Draft (swing keel up/down) | 2'0"/5'0" |
| Draft (fin/wing keel) | 3'6"/2'6" |
| Displacement (swing keel) | 2,290 lbs. |
| Ballast (swing/fin/wing keel) | 452/765/708 lbs. |
| Water (with galley option) | 4.5 gal. |
| Engine (optional) | Outboard |
| Design | CatalinaYachts |
| Price (w/trailer and sails) | ca. $22,000 |

**Catalina 22 Sport**

| | |
|---|---|
| LOA | 23'10" |
| LWL | 19'4" |
| Beam | 7'4" |
| Sail Area (std.) | 205 sq. ft. |
| Draft (board up/down) | 1'8"/5'0" |
| Mast height | 25'0" |
| Displacement | 2,380 lbs. |
| Ballast | 550 lbs. |
| Engine (optional) | Outboard |
| Design | Catalina Yachts |
| Price (w/trailer and sails) | ca. $17,000 |

**Capri 22**

| | |
|---|---|
| LOA | 24'8" |
| LWL | 20'0" |
| Beam | 8'2" |
| Sail Area (std./tall) | 229/255 sq. ft. |
| Draft (wing /fin keel) | 2'8"/4'0" |
| Ballast (wing/fin keel) | 700/650 lbs. |
| Displacement | 2,250/2,200 lbs. |
| Mast height (std./tall) | 31'4"/33'4" |
| Engine (optional) | Outboard |
| Design | Catalina Yachts |
| Price (w/trailer and sails) | ca. $18,500 |

**Catalina 250**

| | |
|---|---|
| LOA | 26'11" |
| LWL | 21'3" |
| Beam | 8'6" |
| Sail Area (std. 100%) | 265 sq. ft. |
| Draft (board up/down/wing keel) | 1'8"/5'9"/3'5" |
| Mast height | 33'3" |
| Displacement (board/wing keel) | 3,250 lbs./ 4,200 lbs. |
| Ballast (board/wing keel) | 1,200 lbs./ 1,050 lbs. |
| Water | 12 gal. |
| Engine (optional) | Yanmar 9-hp. Saildrive/ outboard |
| Design | Catalina Yachts |
| Price (w/trailer and sails) | ca. $31,500 |

Catalina Yachts
21200 Victory Blvd.
Woodland Hills, CA 91367
(818) 884-7700
www.catalinayachts.com

## Com-Pac

Building small boats these days is an economic high-wire act, since the profit margins are razor thin. That means a company has to make a large number of the same vessel, or it has to find a niche with customers who like that company's design and building philosophy and are ready to pay more for the privilege of owning one of their products. Somewhere between these two extremes is Com-Pac Yachts of Clearwater, Florida, a manufacturer that builds up to 120 boats annually from 14 to 35 feet in length. Two Com-Pacs, the **Eclipse** and the **23/IV** fit the parameters. The Com-Pac 25 is trailerable too; however with nearly 5,000 pounds of displacement it is too big a boat. If you like to learn more about this vessel, go to www.com-pacyachts.com.

At less than 21 feet of overall length including bow sprit, the Eclipse is at the short end of our spectrum, but the vessel offers a host of cruisy features in a package that's easy to trailer, launch and store. Shaped with input from naval architect Bruce Bingham the sloop-rigged Eclipse has a touch of tradition in its lines, remotely resembling a New England Catboat with a rounded cabin trunk forward, a plumb stem and a wide stern.

The hull is hand-laid in triaxial fiberglass and polyester resin. The external hull joint is bolted and sealed and capped with a stainless-steel rubrail on the outside. Through-hulls and chainplates have glassed-in plywood backing.

A waterline of more than 18 feet ensures decent performance in a range of conditions. Somehow, Com-Pac coaxed a real boat into this package with nifty ideas that increase livability. Galley, stove and sink are part of an assembly between the two vanities that separate the saloon from the forepeak. The V-berth forward is OK for two adults and two more can squeeze into the convertible saloon berths. Quite frankly, it's going to be tight with four grown-ups in this interior, which has no more than sitting or crouching headroom. Com-Pac says a head fits into this arrangement, but it would have to be a porta-potti and real privacy is not on the options list.

The Eclipse has a flat hull shape under the waterline but extends the maximum beam outboard with soft chines, which add stability. The boat also has 700 pounds of glassed-in interior ballast and a steel centerboard. The relatively long waterline and a

Com-pac Eclipse. The curved sheer and rounded cabin trunk give the Eclipse
a "salty" look that's offset by modern elements such as an open stern.

115-percent genoa sheeted via adjustable cars help the sailing
performance. Standard equipment such as fuel storage locker,
swim ladder and the workable galley arrangement add to the
Eclipse's pocket cruiser status.

Auxiliary propulsion is provided by a small optional outboard that mounts on a bracket on the stern. A fine feature is the
open transom and the unobstructed cockpit, which is made possible by a multi-functional stainless-steel arch that anchors the
mainsheet blocks, serves as bimini attachment and as rig support
for trailering.

The Com-Pac Mastendr system with a pinned mast hinge,

quick-release levers and a stainless-steel strut makes it possible to raise and lower the rig in a jiffy without an army of helpers. The tackle doubles as boom vang.

If going on the road often and doing so with light baggage and no more than one crew or a spouse and two small kids is the chosen form of entertainment, the Eclipse should make the short list. Ditto, if marina fees and flexible access to shallow-water venues are important.

If 20 feet and change of LOA is too compact for your taste, check out the Eclipse's larger sister, the Com-Pac 23/IV. At 3,000 pounds of displacement the fourth edition of this traditional pocket cruiser is 800 pounds heavier, but it's also more ship with a 7-foot-2-inch cockpit, real two-cabin interior and a masthead rig. In contrast to the Eclipse, the 23/IV uses no centerboard, but

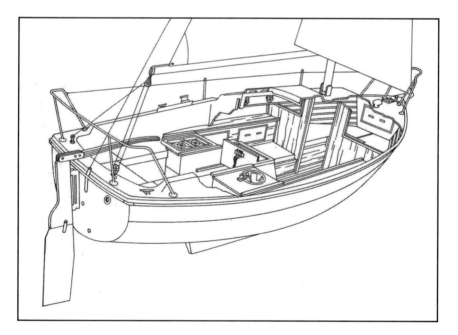

Cutaway drawing of the Com-pac 23/IV.
With 3 more feet LOA than the Eclipse,
the 23/IV is more shippy, but also more boat to handle.

a shallow 2-foot-3-inch keel with wing sections, which saves cabin space but also diminishes the boat's ability to point very high when sailing to weather. In addition to hand-laid glass for the hull laminate, the 23/IV also has longitudinal and transverse stringers that add stiffness to the construction. Six bronze opening ports, lifelines, stainless-steel bow and stern pulpits, anchor roller, a chain locker, an electrical package with interior and navigation lights, good storage and liberal use of wooden trim add to the character of this little cruiser.

If you plan to sail in light to moderate winds, consider an overlapping genoa and an optional roller furling system, so you have more sail to work with, but not enough to be overwhelmed. At the time of this writing, Com-Pac still resisted the in-mast roller-furling trend for the main and offered a jiffy reefing system in the standard sail package for the 23/IV. With its shallow draft this boat will go places that larger vessels with deeper draft won't be able to access and with a dual-axle trailer it will own the road, too.

**Com-Pac Eclipse**

| | |
|---|---|
| LOA | 20'10" |
| LWL | 18'1" |
| Beam | 7'4" |
| Sail Area (std.) | 200 sq. ft. |
| Mast height | 26'0" |
| Draft (board up/down) | 1'6"/5'2" |
| Displacement | 2,200 lbs. |
| Ballast | 700 lbs. |
| Water | 5 gal. |
| Engine (optional) | Outboard |
| Design | Com-Pac Yachts/ Bruce Bingham |
| Price (w/trailer and sails) | ca. $25,000 |

**Com-Pac 23/IV**

| | |
|---|---|
| LOA | 23'11" |
| LWL | 20'2" |
| Beam | 7'10" |
| Sail Area (std.) | 250 sq. ft. |
| Draft | 2'3" |
| Mast height | 30'0" |
| Displacement | 3,200 lbs. |
| Ballast | 1,340 lbs. |
| Water | 10 gal. |
| Engine | Outboard |
| Design | Com-Pac Yachts/Clark Mills |
| Price (w/trailer and sails) | ca. $32,500 |

Com-Pac Yachts
1195 Kapp Dr.
Clearwater, FL 33765
(727) 443-4408
www.com-pacyachts.com

### Etap

For more than 35 years, Belgian manufacturer Etap Yachting has been building yachts that have earned respect for ergonomics, sailing capabilities, building quality and unsinkability. This is not unique to Etap, but it has been marketed successfully as an important safety feature, which appeals to family sailors. Etap calls it the ship-in-ship construction, where deck and hull are double-skinned and the space between the two layers is filled with closed-cell polyurethane foam, which gives the boat sufficient buoyancy to stay afloat even when the water inside is as high as the cabin ceiling. Etap injects foam into the space between the two shells and in areas where it won't cut down on interior space. The company's float tests with open seacocks still generate publicity and have become popular events for the European yachting press. But there are other advantages to a double molded-construction technique, which include sound and temperature insulation, which are notoriously difficult issues on fiberglass boats. It also produces a rigid and stiff hull, which results in better performance.

The **Etap 21i** is offered in two keel versions, a shallow-draft tandem keel and a regular cast-iron fin keel. The boat has a long water line (20 feet) and dual rudders like an Open 60 round-the-world racer, which most American designers seem to avoid, but sailors who have experienced the benefits of dual rudders swear by them, because of the safety aspect and because the boat remains well controllable under heel. The beam is carried far aft, as it is on most modern designs of the early 21st century, so the boat has both lots of stowage space in the cockpit and form stability. A standard sail-area of 257 sq.ft is enough to keep a crew busy in a breeze and definitely suffices for good light-air abilities.

The cabin sleeps four in a saloon that has a small but functional galley, stowage under the long settees and a V-berth forward. The interior is finished in marine ply, which is coated on both sides with a maintenance-free laminate, perhaps a bit pedestrian by Etap's own standards. For their larger models the company has hired the reputable Italian design studio of Bertone to breathe some new life into the rather conservative world of cabin décor and lay-out. Floorboards are removable to allow easy access for inspection of the keel bolts, while the companionway has a foldaway step with a non-slip pad and transparent plexiglas washboards.

When the saloon table is not needed, it disappears under the cockpit or becomes a cockpit table, which is very helpful for an al-fresco dinner. The galley is functional with a two-burner stove, a PVC sink and a manual water pump. Sufficient to prepare a meal and wash up afterwards. The arrangement of the head is simple and basic: a portable or marine toilet in the forepeak, alas adjacent to the galley. An optional roller curtain can be installed for a modicum of privacy.

The deck has plenty of non-skid surfaces and aluminum toe rails that provide safety and support for the crew. These rails also make it easy to tie off fenders and spring lines. The rig tension is taken up by stainless-steel tie rods on the external chainplates.

Etap claims that by mounting chainplates as far outside as possible, it's possible to reduce the rig load that is transferred to the hull by up to 30 percent. The hull-deck joint is both mechanically fastened and chemically bonded and covered by a rub rail.

The wide and spacious cockpit is self-draining and offers stowage for gear on both sides and for the fuel tank under the sole. The double rudder has another advantage: the outboard bracket can be mounted in the center of the stern, which by all accounts is more convenient and efficient for the back that has to lift or lower the engine.

The deck-stepped ⅞-rig with a loose-footed mainsail has one set of aerofoil spreaders and includes a ring to attach the optional spinnaker boom. All standing rigging is made from stainless-steel wire with turnbuckles. The forestay has an adjustable quick-release connection and the boom is fitted with an outhaul and two reefing lines, which can be handled from the cockpit. The boom is

Etap 24. On balmy evenings, the saloon table can move into the cockpit for a civilized al-fresco dinner.

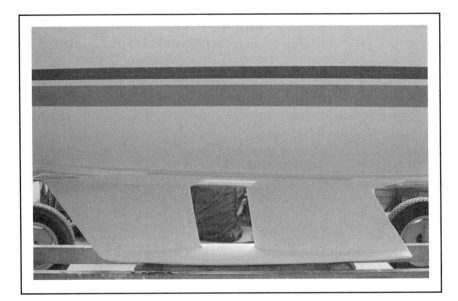

Etap 24's tandem keel opens access to shallow-water venues
while helping the boat to decent upwind performance.

fitted with a vang and the halyards have snap-shackles for easy
sail attachment.

The mainsail has two reef points and a pronounced roach,
which is supported by the two upper full-length battens. The jib is
a 115-percent overlapping headsail, which is a good compromise
that provides enough horsepower in light air while remaining
manageable in a blow.

The standard cast-iron fin keel has a bulb for a low center of
gravity, but the real fun appendage seems to be the slightly heavier tandem keel that reduces draft and thus becomes the ticket to
shallow-draft venues.

The two rudders are connected by a tie-rod and the angle of
the optional lifting rudder blades can be adjusted separately. It's a
must-have option for easy launching and shallow-water operation.

The **Etap 24i** offers more of the same in a seaworthy package that should entice any serious small-boat cruiser, despite two
drawbacks: One is the measurements (ca. 4,000 lbs. of displace-

ment and 8-foot, 3 inches of beam), the second one is the relatively high price, due to exchange rate fluctuation between U.S.
dollar and the Euro.

Comparing the specifications and dimensions of both boats,
the attentive reader will notice that the beam is nearly the same on
the 21i and the 24i, which indicates that the smaller boat has pro-
portionally more volume. One of the pronounced differences between these two models is the interior of the 24i, which has a
"real" galley with a split set up that has the stove to port and the
sink to starboard and a separate head compartment, for which a
plumbed toilet is an option. Another one is the Yanmar 10 hp. inboard diesel, which could be a worthy alternative to an outboard,
especially if you plan on taking this boat to places far afield. An
ergonomic facet that won't go unnoticed by knowledgeable sailors
is the angle of the cockpit coaming that makes it comfortable to sit
on the high side when heeled and steering the boat with the tiller
extension. The smooth transition of the coaming to the coachroof
not only benefits the lines, but it's also an important safety feature
in rough weather. If the boat is fitted with an optional removable
mainsheet traveler (a recommended feature) re-arranging the
cockpit from sailing to party configuration is a snap.

The Etap 24i is an option for couples who want a bit more
legroom than the 21i offers or a family with one or two children. The
boat is certified as Category B, which in EU-speak means coastal
cruising. But if easy trailering and daysailing is your primary concern,
you might want to consider the 21i.

**Etap 21i**

| | |
|---|---|
| LOA | 21'6" |
| LWL | 20'0" |
| Beam | 8'2" |
| Draft (shoal/deep) | 2'4"/4'3" |
| Displacement (shoal/deep) | 2,711 / 2,601 lbs. |
| Ballast (shoal/deep) | 771/661 lbs. |
| Sail Area (main+genoa) | 258 sq. ft. |
| Mast clearance | 34'2" |

| | |
|---|---|
| Water | 5.3 gal. |
| Engine | Outboard |
| Design | Mortain & Mavrikios/ |
| | Etap Yachting NV |
| Price (inc. sails and trailer) | ca. $45,000 |

**Etap 24i**

| | |
|---|---|
| LOA | 26'4" |
| LWL | 22'0" |
| Beam | 8'3" |
| Draft (shoal/deep) | 2'9"/4'11" |
| Displacement (shoal/deep) | 4,008 / 3,964 lbs. |
| Ballast (shoal/deep) | 1,145 /1,101 lbs. |
| Sail Area (main+genoa) | 327 sq. ft. |
| Mast clearance | 38'1" |
| Water | 13 gal. |
| Engine | Outboard or optional |
| | 10-hp. Yanmar diesel |
| Design | M.O. von Ahlen/ |
| | Etap Yachting NV |
| Price (inc. sails and trailer) | ca. $65,000 |

Etap Marine LLC
148 Division Avenue
Summit, NJ 07901
(908) 918-1886
www.etap-usa.com

### Hunter

Hunter Marine, of Alachua, Florida, is known as one of the largest manufacturers of recreational boats in the U.S. with sailboat models that range from dinghies to blue-water cruisers. Regardless of size, Hunter boats emphasize comfort, convenience and ease of use, an approach that resonates with boat buyers.

In the segment of trailerable pocket cruisers, the company has had success with two models, the Hunter 260 and the Hunter 240, which were replaced in 2005 by the **Hunter 25**. Glenn Henderson,

Hunter 25. The Hunter 25 is a big 25-footer that combines stability
with an easy sail plan and generous accommodations.

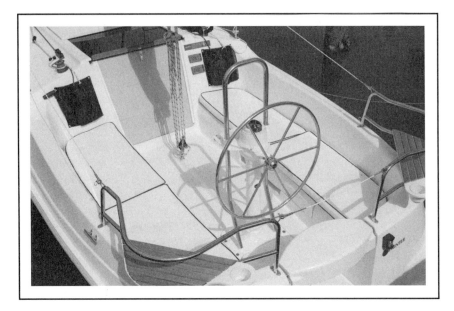

Hunter 25. The large cockpit has enough room for family and friends.
Wheel steering is offered as an option.

who heads the in-house design team, follows the company's promise of delivering a maximum of amenities and comfort in any size boat, while keeping it all simple, easy and fun to operate. The Hunter 25's looks are reminiscent of its predecessors, but a closer examination reveals improvements in many details. "We enhanced the contours, added smoother deck lines, improved the ergonomics and upgraded the accommodations," said Henderson, describing what he thinks is "a great-looking boat that is very easy to sail."

The simple sail plan on a fractional single-spreader aluminum mast includes a roller furled jib and a conventional main with jiffy reefing system. The fiberglass hull accommodates a large teak-trimmed interior, a family-sized cockpit with a wheel, rail seats (both optional) and a walk-through transom that accommodates the outboard bracket, a swim ladder and a swim step. There are no side decks, which forces crew to walk on top of the cabin to get to the foredeck. It's a calculated trade-off for more interior space and

Hunter had the good sense to include lifelines in the standard package. The stern-hung rudder has a lever system to raise and lower the blade, which is a handy feature at the launch ramp.

The boat has a fixed 1,300-pound lead keel that is encased in fiberglass while the hull is still in the mold. It draws only two feet, which makes it possible to launch and sail in shallow water and gives the boat a low profile when it sits on the trailer.

The cabin sleeps four adults in the forward V-berth and the athwartships double berth under the cockpit. It wouldn't be a Hunter if the vessel didn't have a workable galley, an enclosed head compartment with portable toilet (a plumbed marine head with holding tank is optional) and other standard features such as a screened aft-bunk hatch, a teak dining table, galley sink with manual fresh-water pump, portable stove and ice chest. A galvanized dual-axle trailer is standard equipment, but—and that is an important but—you will need a muscular towing vehicle since Hunter lists the towing weight for the package at 4,650 pounds and the width at 8 feet and 5.5 inches.

If small-boat cruising needs to offer more than bare essentials and if boat weight is not a critical issue, the Hunter 25 should be a candidate, especially if access to shallow water is important. Don't get distracted by Hunter's tongue-in-cheek nickname for the 25 "baby cruiser." The boat aims at boaters who want to upgrade from dinghies or other small boats to a comfortable family vessel suitable for weekend cruising and road trips. The other target group includes downsizers, who want a smaller and more flexible package after years of paying ever-increasing slip fees in the same marina.

**Hunter 25**

| | |
|---|---|
| LOA | 24'6" |
| LWL | 22'1" |
| Beam | 8'5 1/2" |
| Sail Area (std. 100%) | 239 sq. ft. |
| Draft (rudder up/down) | 2'0"/2'6" |
| Ballast | 1,309 lbs |
| Displacement | 3,700 lbs |

| Mast Height | 31'8" |
| Water | 10.0 gal |
| Engine (optional) | 10-hp. outboard |
| Price (inc. sails and trailer) | ca. $27,000 |

Hunter Marine
14700 US Highway 441
Alachua, FL, 32615
(386) 462-3077
www.huntermarine.com

### MacGregor

The MacGregor Yacht Corporation has been building trailerable sailboats for more than three decades and claims to be the most innovative company in the industry, having invented the retractable keel and started the trailerable sailboat market. MacGregor is one of the most successful volume builders in the U.S. One of the company's most popular products ("the world's best selling cruising sailboat") is the MacGregor 26, a design by Roger MacGregor that has been around since the 1980s. Over the years it has received upgrades and modifications, which are all incorporated in the current model, the **MacGregor 26M.**

Looking at the images, it is obvious that this boat is very different from traditional sailboats, simply because it is also a powerboat. Traditionalists never embraced it because it is unusual and it is a hybrid, but the market doesn't seem to care. There are plenty of boaters who want to do both, go for a leisurely sail in the morning and have the kids take a spin on water skis in the evening after the wind has shut down, all with the same boat, and all without a lot of fuss.

The MacGregor 26M is built from solid hand-laid fiberglass with a bolted-through hull/deck joint and built-in foam flotation that will keep the vessel afloat in case of damage to the hull. Unlike many other similarly sized boats, this cabin layout is open and the space (6-foot headroom) seems incredibly large, and looks even larger with a rear-facing mirror mounted on the forward

MacGregor 26. Making way under genoa in a gentle breeze.

bulkhead. There are two double berths, one forward of the mast as a V-berth and one aft, under the cockpit. In the saloon, the dinette to starboard converts into a large bunk, while the galley to port slides fore and aft on rails that are recessed into the settee base. So it can be out of the way if space in the saloon is needed for guests. But when the cook needs standing headroom to prepare a sumptuous meal, the entire module emerges from its hiding spot in the aft cabin. When the galley is retracted, access to the rear berth is only possible on starboard, for which the backrest of the dinette's rear seat folds down. The 26M also has an enclosed head, which comes standard with a porta-potti, or optional with a fully plumbed marine toilet and holding tank with overboard discharge.

As a sailboat the MacGregor 26M scores points with features that include a rotating wing mast for more efficient airflow along the mainsail, 1,150 pounds of water ballast that can be filled and

MacGregor 26. In a few minutes the boat is transformed from pocket cruiser to powerboat.

discharged while under way, a completely removable high-aspect ratio daggerboard that can't swivel up upon contact with the bottom or a floating object, twin tilt-up rudders and a large cockpit for operation under power and sail. At the aft end of that cockpit is the helm seat that hinges up and creates a walk-through transom.

Contrary to the previous model the 26X, the 26M also has 300 pounds of extra internal lead ballast, which makes the boat a bit heavier to tow, but certainly improves its upwind sailing potential. The draft with board up is one foot and extends to 5 feet 9 inches with board down. This also permits the boat to sit very low on its trailer and makes it fairly easy to launch. The shallow underbody makes quick turns easier under motor and facilitates beaching.

Unlike other boats in this class that use 4 to 10-hp. auxiliary engines, the MacGregor 26M is designed to handle outboards that make it possible to get on a plane and tow a water skier. According to the company's Web site, the boat will manage 22 mph with a 50-hp engine. MacGregor reported that some owners go with 70-hp. or even larger engines.

The metamorphosis from sail to power is simple: Douse the canvas and tie it up well, raise the daggerboard, disconnect the steering, flip up the twin rudders and connect the steering to the outboard. Turn the key and take command with the wheel and throttle at the steering pedestal. As a father of two sons, I can remember that when they entered their teens they, like the rest of their friends, found going fast to be more exciting than going slow. I mention this to suggest that the powerboat feature of the Mac-Gregor 26M may serve to keep your teenage children interested and to maintain boating as an activity for the whole family.

If the boat has been sailing, it will be necessary to drain the ballast tank by opening the discharge valve on the transom and going at least 6 knots for a few minutes. The ballast water can also be drained at the launch ramp, which is the key to having a light boat on the trailer. That is a distinct advantage over boats that feature heavy fixed keels.

MacGregor 26. The mirror behind the table and the sliding galley (left foreground) make the interior look and feel bigger than it really is.

This is what renowned yacht designer Bob Perry has to say about the MacGregor 26M and its unusual appearance, "I wouldn't put this boat alongside the latest Chuck Paine design and compare the aesthetics. The 26 shows a hybrid power/sail look that won't work on many boats. The wraparound windows and lack of side decks are right out of the powerboat school. I think you have to put this boat into an aesthetics genre of its own, [but] all the proportions are there for a decent sailing boat."

**MacGregor 26M**

| | |
|---|---|
| LOA | 25'10" |
| LWL | 23'2" |
| Beam | 7'9" |
| Sail Area (Main and Jib) | 300 sq. ft. |
| Displacement | 2,550 lbs. |
| Ballast | 1,450 lbs. (1,150 lbs. water, 300 lbs. Lead) |
| Trailer Weight | 710 lbs. |
| Draft (board up/down) | 1'0"/ 5'9" |
| Mast Height (above deck) | 30'0" |
| Water | 5 gal. |
| Engine (optional) | 5 to 50 hp. outboard |
| Design | Roger MacGregor |
| Price (Include. trailer and sails) | ca. $21,000 |

Mac Gregor Yacht Corporation
1631 Placentia
Costa Mesa, CA, 92627
(949) 642 6830
www.macgregor26.com

Rhodes (General Boats)

Way past age 45, the **Rhodes 22** seems to have forgotten when it was designed, as it continues to attract a loyal and outspoken following. Built and sold directly by General Boats in Edenton, North Carolina, this Phil Rhodes design with flared-out topsides and nearly absurdly large self-draining cockpit (7-foot-4-inches by 8 feet!) makes no pretense about being modern. But it has remained true to its mission, which was, is and forever shall be: Simple cruising in relative comfort for a couple or a small family. From the deep blue ocean to the shallow coves, a Rhodes 22 covers it all.

The hull is solid hand-laid fiberglass, while deck and cabin top use sandwich-construction. General Boats builds many components from molds, which brings about finished surfaces inside compartments and hatches. Hull and deck are joined over a vertical flange, screwed, glued and covered with a rub rail. Built-in foam makes the boat virtually unsinkable, which offers peace of mind should the hull sustain severe damage. The molded-in keel contains 700 pounds of ballast and the trunk for the pivoting centerboard that extends the boat's draft to four feet when fully deployed.

The unusually spacious cockpit has open-front seating, which is comfortable for the legs because they can be tucked back under the seat and still leave space to stow bins that hold assorted items, which won't fit into the lazarette. This area of the boat can be an extension to the cabin if an optional boom tent ("boom room" in Rhodes-speak) is rigged.

To hold up the rig no fewer than nine stays are used on the Rhodes 22, which by modern standards is overkill. However, by conservative safety measures that's very solid, as a broken forestay might not automatically result in a downed rig. The folks in Edenton try to convince prospective buyers of the virtues of in-mast furling and to a certain degree they are right: A vertically furled mainsail is easy to reduce in size and to put away. It is a consideration for short- or single-handed sailing. But from a pure performance standpoint a conventionally rigged mainsail with a jiffy reef still is the connoisseurs' choice, since it is bigger, it has horizontal battens to keep the sail in better shape, and it's more efficient in light air or when going to weather. Owners can also choose from a small 100-sq.ft. standard jib or a 175% roller-furling genoa of twice that size, depending on their sailing style and venue(s). Some owners like a 150-percent genoa better, because a 200-squarefoot sail on such a small boat is unwieldy and needs to be furled up early to prevent overpowering.

Rhodes 22. Pop-top, roller furling, bimini and large cockpit make this
design a perennial favorite with small-boat cruisers.

Alternatively, the factory offers a smaller, self-tending jib that approximately resembles a staysail.

Below deck, the Rhodes 22 pretends to be bigger than it is on
the outside, which is a feat that tiny sub-compact cars seem to have
learned from this boat. The large cockpit is not compatible with
quarter berths, which is not necessarily a detriment. Instead a very
functional fixed galley, a convertible dinette and a fully enclosed
and plumbed head were fitted into the saloon. Forward, a 6-foot
V-berth accommodates short adults or the kids, while taller folks
will stay in the saloon. The secret for this bonanza of space is found
in the small overhangs on bow and stern and the well-used beam. In
addition, the boat has a pop-top that lifts up on telescoping arms and
locks automatically in any desired position. This feature extends the
headroom in the saloon either by a few inches or all the way to 6
feet, 4 inches. Best of all: the boat sails with the top up.

For motorization, Rhodes offers a smart package with a sliding outboard bracket that is somewhat more sophisticated than the adjustable aluminum brackets you buy off the shelf someplace. And a 10-hp. four-stroke should provide plenty of push for 2,900-pounds of displacement.

Under sail, she won't break records, but that's not the chief rationale to go sailing on a trailerable cruiser anyway. A PHRF rating of 258 puts the Rhodes 22 slightly ahead of a Columbia 22 and in the ballpark of other small cruisers of that era. Little wetted surface and a long waterline helps light-air performance and shifting gears is made easy by sail control lines that are led aft to the cockpit. A little curious but practical nonetheless, is the traveler's position between the stanchions of the sternrail, where it is out of the way so the big cockpit remains undivided.

Reviewers have commented on the lack of a boom vang to shape the main on a reach or downwind, and molded-in footrests

Rhodes 22. With traveler and mainsheet out of the way, the cockpit converts into a gigantic double berth or a party space.

on the cockpit floor to give the crew a bracing point when the boat is heeled over. Adding either one or both sounds like an easy owner's upgrade.

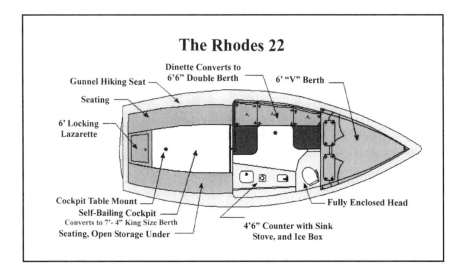

There is an active and enthusiastic owner's community, dubbed the "Rowdy Rhodies," that communicates through an e-mailing list that covers all things Rhodes 22 and then some (rhodes22-list@rhodes22.org). The factory also offers refurbished used boats (a sort of buyback/upgrade program) and a loaner option for newcomers who like to try now and perhaps buy later. The magazine *Practical Sailor* notes that the Rhodes 22 ". . . packs a lot of cruising capability into a small trailerable boat."

**Rhodes 22**

| | |
|---|---|
| LOA | 22'0" |
| LWL | 20'0" |
| Beam | 8'0" |
| Sail Area (std./175% genoa) | 210/300 sq. ft. |
| Displacement | 3,200 lbs. |
| Ballast | 700 lbs. |
| Draft (board up/down) | 1'8"/ 4'0" |

| Mast clearance | 26'0" |
| Fresh-water Capacity | 15 gal. |
| Engine (optional) | 10 hp. outboard |
| Price (inc. sails and trailer) | ca. $45,000 |

General Boats
114 Midway Dr.
Edenton, NC 27932
(252) 482-4372
www.rhodes22.com

### Santana (W.D. Schock Corp.)

The Schock history is typical for the California of the post-war years. Barely in his teens W. D. "Bill" Schock built a boat in the garage of his family's home. After World War II, he moved into a small beach house in Newport Beach and did odd boat-building jobs while working on a cold-molded International 14 for himself. But before he could finish it, someone made him an offer and his decision to sell put W. D. Schock Corp. on the map. The timing was perfect because the fiberglass boat-building revolution was about to roll over Southern California, following that state's boom-and-bust principle. But Schock survived and today Sabots, Lido 14s, Harbor 20s, Schock 35s and the revolutionary Schock 40 with canting keel are in production. Over the years, the company has built more than 13,000 boats from 70 different designs.

In 1965, Bill's oldest son, Tom, met budding designer Gary Mull. Together they developed the Santana 22, a trailerable pocket racer/cruiser. With durability, good sailing qualities—especially in a breeze—basic accommodations for a couple or a small family this boat helped lure a whole generation into the sport. It was Mull's first big success and it helped establish Schock in the market of trailerable sailboats. The Santana 22 quickly became popular on San Francisco Bay and other windy venues such as Monterey, Oklahoma, the Columbia River, Houston, Dallas, and

Lake Dillon, Colorado. A total of 747 boats were built in the first production run, and many of them still sail today.

Motivated by an order for six boats in 2001, Schock decided to revitalize the **Santana 22** with the input from existing owners. The vessel was brought up to the 21st-century expectations and still complies to the one-design rules of the existing Santana 22 class. Nostalgia certainly played a role in this— the remake of the Santana 22 remained faithful to its original design principles. Besides cosmetics and trim, the upgrades include better deck hardware (e.g. stainless-steel chainplates instead of aluminum and a Harken traveler), a molded-in toe rail on the foredeck, a stronger hull/deck joint and internal components, a larger stern cutout for modern 4-stroke outboards, a sturdier boom and halyards led inside the mast. According to the company, all these additions still don't make the new boat heavier than the old ones, which is a credit to modern building technology.

One-design or PHRF racing and spirited daysailing are the strengths of this vessel, but there are also plenty of cruising yarns,

Santana 22. Upgraded in 2001, this evergreen offers good
sailing qualities and active fleets in many places.

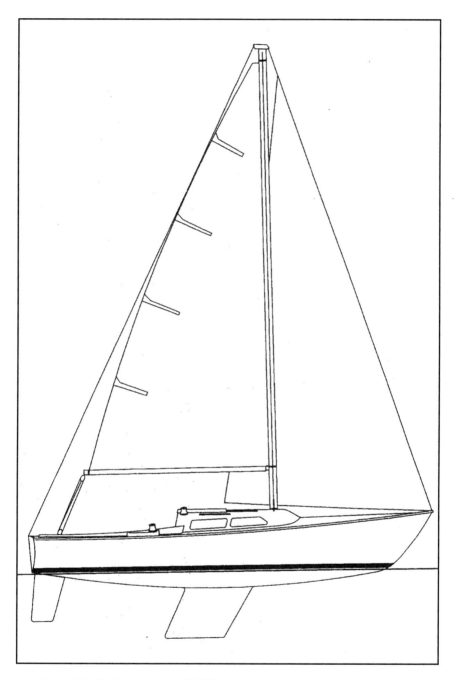

Santana 22. The lines betray her mid-1960s vintage, but on the water that is of no concern.

such as this one: "I rebuilt a Santana 22, including broken rudder and mast on Guam and sailed it thousands of miles in the Northern Marianas and Guam waters. I had more adventures on that small boat than I did on a host of larger boats I have sailed all over the Western Pacific. I went through a typhoon at sea with her and numerous rough-water events. I even used her to carry cargo to the inhabitants of Alamagan and Agrighan after the converted fishing boat that serviced them was lost at sea. We loaded until water started coming in the cockpit drains and then set sail from Saipan. On our return runs, I carried betel nut, dried fish and glass balls. She drove like an old Toyota truck and could take much more than I could stand . . ."

While this never was the intended use of a Santana 22, the boat's handling and its ability to take a beating have helped this sailor come through his adventures alive. Mull's hull design has a fine entry, which helps windward performance and beam that's carried aft, which increases stability. Other keys to the boat's success are the large, self-bailing cockpit and the masthead rig that accommodates a variety of sail configurations.

The hull construction on the Santana 22 is hand-laid fiberglass with reinforcements in high-stress areas. The 1,230-pound cast-iron keel is fixed, which increases stability with a low center of gravity and opens up the interior because no trunk and lifting mechanism are required. Unlike most other boats, the Santana has a spade rudder that is attached to the underside of the hull. It is made of laminated fiberglass with a stainless-steel shaft and a wooden tiller.

Schock found a decent compromise with the deck so it doesn't completely sacrifice cabin space while it fits well with the proportions of the boat. The deck is made of sandwich laminate with end-grain balsa core and critical areas are reinforced with additional fiberglass or plywood. The molded cockpit coaming integrates with the deck. The walking areas are non-skidded and the 8-foot long cockpit offers enough space for four to six adults. Large seat hatches open access to the storage lockers underneath.

The overlapping headsail is trimmed with cabin-top winches

and the jib leads are adjustable. An optional bracket can be installed to put the sail control lines within reach of the crew. The main sheet is trimmed with a ratchet block/cam cleat combination that's mounted on a Barney post while a Harken traveler takes care of fine-tuning the mainsail. At the launch ramp, the hinged mast can be quickly stepped and unstepped.

The accommodations are inviting, thanks to the use of teak. The V-berth (for the kids), the saloon berths (for two adults) and the cabin sole are all part of one structure that's bonded to the hull to add stiffness and strength. The main bulkhead is fastened to the interior structure and bonded to hull and deck. The backrests also act as fiddles for loose stuff like bags, crockery and other cabin flotsam. A portable toilet can be fitted in the forward cabin and an ice chest doubles as companionway step.

Compared to the other boats discussed here, the Santana 22 is perhaps the "raciest one" (the original rule was called Midget Ocean Racing Class or MORC) and has spawned a very active class organization (www.santana22.com). Seeing these boats battle big winds and choppy seas in an ebb on the south shore of Angel Island, in San Francisco Bay, makes it clear why they still have their fans.

**Santana 22**

| | |
|---|---|
| LOA | 22' 0" |
| LWL | 18' 8" |
| Beam | 7' 10" |
| Draft | 3' 6" |
| Sail area | 217 sq. ft. |
| Ballast | 1,230 lbs. |
| Displacement | 2,600 lbs. |
| Designer | Gary Mull |
| Price (w/ sails and trailer) | $33,000 |

W.D.Schock Corp.
23125 Temescal Canyon Road
Corona, CA 92883
(951) 277-3377
www.santanasailboats.com

## ➤ SUMMARY ◄

If your profession, your family, and other factors permit month-long coastal or ocean cruises, by all means get a boat in the 30- to 45-foot range. But remember that when you are not cruising, you still own that boat, which means you have to pay for the cost incurred. You may have to leave it in a marina berth that will continue to go up in rent. Perhaps the marina is hours away and commuting to the boat will take time out of your schedule that you could use much better for sailing. If your sailing will be limited to local waters, consider sailing big on a trailerable sailboat. You can keep it in your own backyard, or at a local storage lot, plus you have the benefit of a boat that will go on the road with you, should you want a change of venue.

If you want to have some fun, try and run the numbers. Add up purchase price (plus interest if you need to finance it), monthly storage cost, estimated annual maintenance, fuel etc. Then divide that by the number of days or hours you spend (or intend to spend) sailing. A vessel that costs $5,000 to maintain per year and gets sailed once or twice is more expensive than the occasional charter where you drop the sails, tie up at the dock and walk away.

Read the chapter about buying used before you settle on a strategy. A project boat could be a great deal and there are countless vintage Santana 22s, Catalina 22s, Rhodes 22s etc. to be found. However, be reasonable about assessing value to your spare time and your skills as an amateur shipwright. A surprisingly accurate rule to remember is that most boat projects spiral into something much bigger. They tend to take twice as long and twice the money that was originally budgeted. Some jobs may be over your head, which means you have to hire professional help. And at $80-100 per hour for a specialist's time that exercise can become expensive. If you want to balance maintenance with tiller time, you might want to consider buying new or a newer model that is well maintained. Check the resources at the end of Chapter 8 before you start your research.

# 2
# *Sails and Motors*

*The forces at work are the same for any size sail-boat, be they eight or 80 feet in length.*

E.S. MALONEY, Chapman Piloting

## ➢ SAILS ≺

Aside from the hull, the most important and most expensive items on a sailboat are the sails, the primary source of propulsion. Trimming them properly makes a sailing vessel move through the water efficiently.

There are many different sails especially since asymmetrical spinnakers have become the rage, but for a primer we will limit our discussion to the four most basic ones, the main, the jib, the genoa, and the symmetrical spinnaker.

Sailmaking technology like other aspects of yacht design has evolved and become sophisticated, which has resulted in lighter and more efficient sails. Computers have long been part of this process in designing, cutting, and sewing sails from woven Dacron panels. Dacron is still a popular material, but nowadays performance-hungry customers are often contemplating the purchase of three-dimensionally thermo-molded sails that are produced with aramid fibers under vacuum pressure with adhesives instead of stitches at the seams.

This technology seems to be creeping into the mainstream and trickling down to smaller boats. Without going into too much detail, the advantage of laminated sails is their lightness and their ability to hold their shape longer over a broader range of conditions, which helps performance. The downside is the higher price and that they are less tolerant of abuse and exposure to sunlight. If you are interested in finding out more, consult with a sailmaker.

Most manufacturers will pepper you with head-spinning names of their products and manufacturing techniques and provide a quote for laminated sails and a comparison number for the same sail made the old-fashioned way from Dacron and with a sewing machine.

### The Mainsail

Of the four basic sail types, the mainsail is the primary engine on modern sailboats (Figure 2-1). It attaches to the rear of the mast at the *luff,* and to the boom at the *foot.* In general, the sail is inserted into grooves in the mast and boom, being held in place by slides or, in some cases, *boltropes.* Boats with full-battened mainsails use little sliders either inside the mast track or on ball bearings that move up and down on a special external track on the back of the mast, which is a bit more complex than the traditional setup but greatly reduces friction and the effort for hoisting a main.

The trailing edge of the sail is called the *leech.* To help the sail hold its shape, *battens* are inserted into pockets that are sewn into the leech of the sail. There are reinforced eyelets at the tack and clew of the sail to attach them to the gooseneck fitting at the front and to the outhaul at the back end of the boom with a shackle. The halyard used to hoist the main is shackled to the headboard. The mainsail can also have eyelets sewn at two different levels across the width of the sail for reefing when the wind picks up. Hence, these eyelets are called *reef points.*

Because the main is the principal sail on a trailerable sailboat, it is used in a wide variety of wind conditions, which makes it subject to a lot of stress and strain. If it's supposed to last, it needs some basic care to maintain its strength and shape. It's not difficult to do and here are a few simple suggestions:

- Ultra-violet radiation degrades fabric and yarn, so keep the sail out of the sun when not in use, either with a boom cover or by taking it off and stowing it in a dry, cool place.

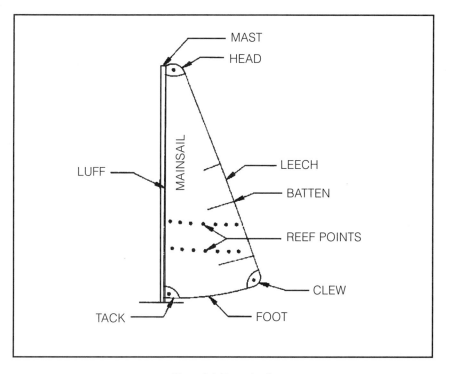

Figure 2-1. The mainsail

Many sailors simply put their sails into the cabin when they don't intend to use their boat for a while, which is better than stowing them in the open, but not ideal.

- Check the stitching in the seams frequently and repair broken threads.
- Watch for wear in the area where it rubs against spreaders, shrouds, lifelines, or lifeline stanchions.
- Keep the sail clean by occasionally hosing it off with fresh water and allowing it to dry. If you sail in saltwater, it is particularly important to wash the sail because salt granules embedded in the fabric attract moisture when it is stored. Be absolutely sure the sail is completely dry before storing, or you will find yourself engaged in a hopeless battle with mold and mildew.

- Don't use any aggressive cleaning agents or bleach to remove mildew, rust or other stains because they will do more harm than good. Swallow your pride and embrace those imperfections as character.

### The Jib

The jib is often also referred to as the headsail. The lower forward corner is called the tack, which is shackled to the stemhead fitting. The narrow upper end is the head, which is shackled to the jib halyard for hoisting it and the sheets are attached to the clew. Regular jibs are attached to the forestay either with hanks or a zippered sleeve hanked. Increasingly, though, that is old style. Most manufacturers offer trailerable cruising boats with a standard or optional roller furling mechanism, which makes short work of deploying and stowing the headsail by wrapping or unwrapping it around the headstay (see Chapter 3 for a more detailed discussion).

Roller furling or not, as you can see from Figure 2-2, unlike a genoa that deeply overlaps the headsail, a working jib has less square footage of sail area than the main. Even if it is hanked on, a jib is not much trouble to put on or take off, so I take it down when I'm done sailing and store it inside the cabin in a sail bag. Just in case you wonder, here are some thoughts about extending the useful life of a headsail:

- Rinse off dirt and salt after use.
- Never fold a regular jib after you've taken it off the boat. Roll it horizontally from the head to the foot and store it in a dry, cool place.
- Don't stow it when it is wet or moist.
- Use a protective bag.
- If your boat has a roller furling jib, makes sure the sail is dry before you furl it if you don't plan on using the sail for a while.

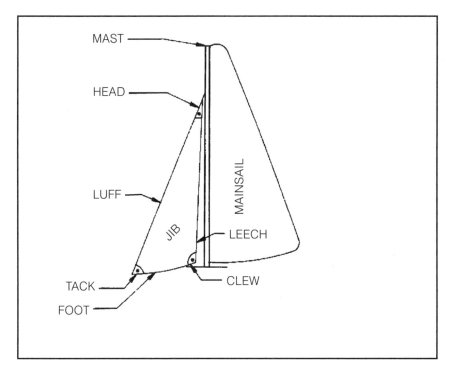

Figure 2-2. The jib

- To prevent a roller furled jib from UV exposure, look into canvas covers that can be hoisted and zippered.

Before we move on to the genoa and spinnaker, let me share some thoughts about buying additional sails. Most trailerable sailboats are delivered with a mainsail and a standard working jib, and that is fine for the beginning. I think you should acquaint yourself with the boat using only these two sails. Not only are genoas and spinnakers expensive, they are much larger sails and require more effort to handle, not to mention more experience to use properly. After you have become comfortable mastering main and jib, there is still plenty of time to add larger and more specialized sails. A smaller sail area will be easier and safer to handle, which translates into more comfort and fun.

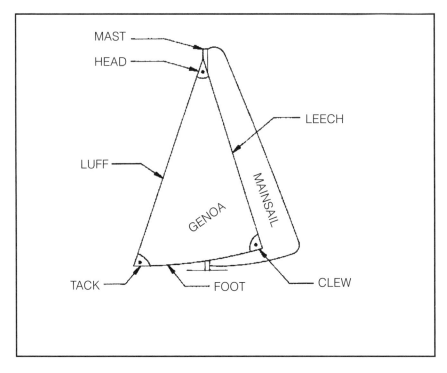

Figure 2-3. The genoa

## The Genoa

A headsail that overlaps the mast and part of the mainsail is called a genoa (Figure 2-3). It has more sail area than the working jib, and is most helpful in lighter air. However, it needs to come down and be replaced by a working jib when the wind pipes up and the boat becomes overpowered. On the other hand, if the boat is equipped with a roller furling system, a genoa can become a jib in the matter of seconds, simply by rolling it up to a smaller size that makes the boat more comfortable to sail. The sizes of genoas often are expressed by a percentage figure that informs how much larger the genoa is relative to a non-overlapping headsail (also called a 100-percent jib). For example, a 105-percent genoa only slightly overlaps the mainsail, whereas a 155-percent genoa is a designated light-air sail that goes farther back on the side deck. These sails are mostly options on trailerable sailboats, but well worth considering because being underpowered in light air is more frequent than being overpowered in a blow. Put it on you list of must-have gear when you are comfortable with main and jib.

### The Spinnaker

A spinnaker is a downwind sail, not unlike a balloon, mostly colorful and made of very light material, such as rip-stop nylon. Flown forward of the mast and in place of—or sometimes along with—the jib or genoa, a spinnaker is designed primarily to enhance the downwind or reaching performance (Figure 2-4). The

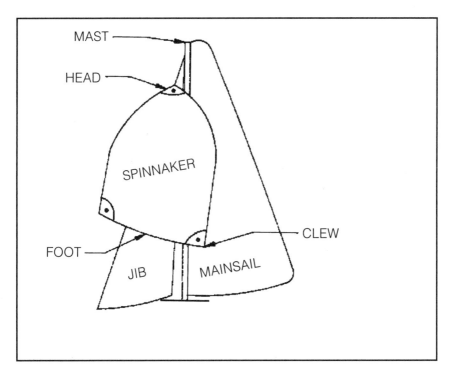

Figure 2-4. The spinnaker

luff on a spinnaker is the windward edge of the sail, and the leech is the leeward edge. Spinnakers can roughly be divided into symmetricals that need a pole that's attached to the mast to fly properly, and asymmetricals that are flown from a bowsprit (on very sporty boats) or from a tack line that's attached to a strong fitting on the bow.

While symmetrical spinnakers are more complex to rig and handle, they allow boats to sail straight downwind. Their asymmetrical cousins are easier to gybe (no "pole dance" required on the foredeck) but with their flatter profile and their way of being flown on the side of the boat rather than out front, they require a "hotter angle," meaning the boat has to sail closer to the wind. Spinnakers like all other gear on a sailboat have made tremendous strides toward usability, so they no longer can be considered racing-only sails. Many small-boat cruisers swear by them as important light-air sails. However, it's true that they are much larger and more demanding of crew work than a jib or a genoa, so some experience is necessary before starting to experiment with them.


## ➤ SUMMARY ≺

I would bet that the majority of drivers don't know a whole lot about how the motor in their car is put together or about aerodynamic principles of the body. Most of us don't worry too much about those things and are content to do the routine maintenance because that keeps it running like it's supposed to run. I found this approach to be convenient for cars and applicable to the sails on my boat.

I can't design sails or sew them together in a way that enhances their durability in the face of stress and strain. Just as I can drive my car, however, I can trim the sails and make the boat go. I can also care for my sails and prolong their useful life. Just do the basic sail maintenance sails, know what canvas to use when, and trim it properly. It will go a long way toward enjoying years of service from a basic set of Dacron sails.

## ➤ MOTORS ➤

People go sailing for a lot of different reasons: In search of freedom, adventure, and solitude, to commune with nature, or to develop self-reliance. In doing all of these things, sailors take great pride in the fact that our sport is one that exists in harmony with nature. In addition to these reasons, many of us are attracted to the quiet elegance and beauty of sailing. But there are limits to peace and zero emissions.

Just take a look at any busy marina at the height of the season. How in the world are those boats going to sail away from such crowded slips? In particular, how are the sailboats that are tied up stern-out going to sail away? You guessed it, they're not. They will crank their motors, shatter the quiet, and putter out of the marina into an open area where they can hoist their sails.

Because internal combustion engines are a source of pollution, no matter how environmentally friendly the brochures claim they are, many sailors have a love-hate relationship with them, knowing that it isn't in the spirit of the sport to use an "iron genny," but also being acutely aware of their practicality and usefulness. In addition to helping exit and re-enter a crowded marina or mooring area, they are great to have when the wind completely disappears. Starting your motor will give you real pleasure on a humid, 95-degree, sun-drenched day when the breeze has shut off while there are still a few miles between you and the next dock or anchorage.

And what about those days when the wind really picks up, the swells begin to grow in size, the spray begins to fly, and crashing through them under sail becomes a bone-shattering, nerve-rattling experience? Well, it could be a comfort to douse the canvas, start the motor, and head in. Besides, it is also nice to have the ability to motor into some out-of-the-way slough or cove.

### Inboard or outboard?

Many of the boats we are discussing in this book are too small for an inboard engine, but from 24 feet on up, a small one-cylinder diesel can be ordered as an option. Some advantages diesels hold over outboards:

- They are more fuel efficient
- They offer better distribution of power, because the propeller doesn't surface in a seaway
- They allow for better weight distribution because the engine block is mounted low and forward near the center of gravity.

Of course there are some drawbacks to consider: If something goes wrong with an inboard diesel, you need to be a mechanic or hire one. Working on an engine inside a small boat usually is no fun, so mechanics who are used to engine rooms with standing headroom might not want to do it, or charge extra. And finally, nothing will inflate the price of a new boat quicker than an optional inboard diesel.

Outboards too, have had to clean up their act. Tighter emission standards by the EPA and many state legislatures have banned the regular carbureted two-stroke outboard. It was inefficient and a gross polluter, dispersing a mixture of unburned fuel and motor oil in the environment. Low initial cost and light weight of regular two-stroke engines were not sufficient arguments to avert their demise. Marine retailers sell off old stock of their two-strokes and there are hundreds of thousands of those engines already in use. But the future belongs to the four-stroke outboard, which is rapidly becoming the norm everywhere because it reduces air pollution by about 75 percent and discharges drastically less unburned gasoline into the water. Four-strokes are not as noisy and offer up to 40 percent better fuel economy over a common two-stroke of comparable size.

### Horsepower

While a 5-hp. outboard motor will move any of the popular trailer-able sailboats along fairly nicely at full throttle, I recommend a stronger motor because you can get the same speed while running at about half-throttle. If you run a 10-hp. motor at wide-open throttle, a 5-hp. outboard cannot keep up. This can make a difference.

One hellishly hot summer day I had been sailing on the Intracoastal Waterway, along with three other boats, when the breeze completely vanished. Because we were about seven miles from our destination, we decided to motor back to the marina. The other three boats had 10-hp. motors, but I only had a five. You can guess the rest. My colleagues took off like bats out of hell and left me in their wake. When I finally arrived, I was hooted and cheered.

More horsepower means more expense, but convenience and extra power when needed are worth something. In addition, I think it would be unseemly to outfit your trailerable sailboat to sail "big" in every way, and then equip it with an underpowered motor. Initially, boaters were concerned about the weight of four-stroke outboards, but engineering ingenuity found an answer to that. Most manufacturers have lightweight motors in their program, ideal as an auxiliary for the inflatable or a small trailerable cruiser. A 6-hp. Mercury four-stroke motor weighs approximately 55 pounds, while a 9.9-hp. model weighs 84 pounds.

Regardless of the power of the motor you put on your stern, you need to make certain that it has forward, neutral, and reverse gears. In addition, you should plan to have an extra gas tank for those occasions when you may be required to power for an extended period of time. Running out of fuel a long way from landfall is no joy. An electric starter would be a nice accessory, and you are more likely to find one on a 10-hp. outboard than on a 5-hp. motor.

### Shaft Length and Motor Brackets

If your boat requires an outboard motor bracket on the transom, it will be important for you to own a motor with a long shaft (usually 20 inches), so that the prop won't come out of the water when motoring through steep seas or swells.

If your boat doesn't have a motor well (which some do) and you want to install an outboard, buy a high-quality outboard motor mount or bracket, and make certain it will fit the angle of your boat's transom. Refer to the boat manufacturer's options list to find the appropriate model. Also be sure that the bracket locks in an up or down position and that it's made of stainless steel with an adequately thick mounting board. A good option is an adjustable outboard engine mounts with torsion springs so the engine can be lifted up easily. This might be your best bet if your transom does not allow tilting the engine when it's not in use. To keep your engine in your possession, consider an outboard motor lock.

## ➢ SUMMARY ≺

Don't automatically buy an outboard motor from your sailboat dealer. Instead, shop around. Lots of businesses sell outboard motors, and you may be able to make a deal that is better than what your boat seller can offer. Again, resist the temptation to buy an old polluter on the cheap. Instead, consider the benefits of a four-stroke and think of it as a critical equipment that can save the day in an emergency.

I also recommend that you visit the nearest marina and talk with the owners about the outboard motors they have on their sailboats. Ask them about ease of starting, how it moves the boat, and fuel efficiency. More importantly, ask them if they would buy the same motor again. If they say no, ask what they would buy, and why. It sure helps to learn from the mistakes of other people instead of making your own.

# 3

# *Deck and Cockpit*

*Comfort is not a measureable quality, mainly because it means different things to different people. It also changes according to the weather, the time of year, the size of the boat, the distance from land, the prevalence of seasickness, and the state of the drinks locker.*

IAN NICOLSON, Comfort in the Cruising Yacht

## ➤ INTRODUCTION ◄

Considering the various layouts and arrangements of a trailerable sailboat, bear in mind that a number of factors contribute to sailing big. When viewed by a non-sailor from the dock, the occupants of a well-sailed boat heeling to a gentle breeze appear relaxed, enjoying themselves, and perhaps sipping something cool. While the observation may be correct, the fact that the sailors are relaxed is not an accident. In this chapter we will consider some of the factors that increase the comfort on a small cruising boat to a level that belies its size.

## ➤ DECK LAYOUT ◄

Deck layout refers to everything above the gunwales, but mostly to the surface of the deck itself. Essentially, there are two configurations we can talk about—a deck with a traditional trunk cabin, or one with a flush deck design. There are several things to consider here, including which look appeals to you the most.

In addition to offering a more traditional look, a trunk cabin creates a little space to move forward and aft between the sides of the cabin and the gunwales of the boat. Some sailors argue that even a narrow walking space is important when one has to go forward to work on the foredeck or at the mast, especially in a seaway or when the boat is heeled over. Blue-water sailors like to point out that this configuration provides a path with secure places to hold on, e.g. to handrails on the cabin top and to lifelines on the outboard side. However, for someone like me, with size 12 feet, the space might get tight on a boat that is fairly small, so some practice will be necessary to become sure-footed.

The flush deck design extends the interior space and headroom all the way to the hull's topsides, which adds to the creature comforts below; however when the boat heels, walking forward and working on the cabintop can be a challenge. There are no handrails to grab. About the only thing you can do under such circumstances is to grab the shrouds or the mast or install sturdy lifelines along the perimeter of the deck.

### ➤ BOW PULPITS AND STERNRAILS ≺

These are two pieces of equipment I consider necessities for sailing big. Bow pulpits prevent you from falling in the water when working on the foredeck, e.g. during a sail change or an anchoring maneuver. They also give you something to grab onto if you should slip or fall. Bow pulpits should be made of ⅞- or 1-inch stainless steel tubes with proper welds. Most manufacturers offer the right kind of pulpits and pushpits if they are not part of the standard equipment. Equally important is the method of attachment of pulpits to the deck, which should have through bolts and a strong adhesive, so they are strong enough to withstand the shock load of a 200-pound body being thrown against them.

On the other end of the boat, sternrails or pushpits serve the same function, keeping people on the boat when sitting in the aft end of the cockpit. Besides, sternrails are also practical for other purposes, as a backrest or a place to stow a throwable flotation device, such as an O ring or a Lifesling in a convenient spot if it is needed in an emergency. Sternrails are also a fine place to mount more mundane devices such as drink holders, a boat barbecue, the flagstaff for the ensign, or the antenna for the VHF radio or GPS transmitter.

## ➤ LIFELINES ◄

In theory lifelines are designed to help keep you on the boat. Practically, however, the lifelines one usually finds on small boats—and on many bigger boats—will serve their theoretical purpose only if you are a child or a very small adult. If you are a normal-size adult, these accessories will usually rise to about knee level. If you are six feet or more, they will strike you slightly below the knees, in just the right place to trip you up.

To make practical sense, lifelines should be at least 24 inches high and they should be solidly installed, bolted through like pulpit and sternrails. Otherwise, they are mostly cosmetic, helping to make a boat look "finished" and providing a place to hang fenders and wet towels. Most trailerable cruising boats don't have lifelines in their standard equipment, so they have to be retrofitted. Whether or not to install them should not be a decision about looks, but about crew safety and it depends on the intended use of the boat and the sailing venues.

## ➤ HATCHES ◄

Hatches are lids on the exterior of the boat that lead to the cabin area, to anchor lockers, or to storage areas in the cockpit. On the boats we are concerned with, there are usually two hatches giving access to the cabin, the companionway hatch and the foredeck hatch. The companionway hatch slides on cabintop runners so it completely covers the companionway when closed. When opened it is pushed forward toward the mast, opening the cabin to additional light and air. The foredeck hatch is located on the forward portion of the cabin or on the foredeck. These hatches are designed to increase light and airflow through the cabin when open. Foredeck hatches can also be used to gain access to the foredeck from the V-berth when necessary.

Hatches need to fit tightly with the surrounding part of the boat and should have adequately deep and properly contoured drainways to keep them from leaking. It is no fun to walk on a wet interior carpet or to try to sleep on a V-berth that is soaked from rain or spray that found its way into the boat. All hatches that raise and lower should be attached with hinges that are through-bolted and not mounted with self-tapping screws. Regardless of the material they are made of (mostly Lexan), deck hatches should have a strong aluminum frame that makes them sturdy enough for an adult to walk or sit on. Foredeck hatches need to have a telescope strut so you can open them as much or as little as you want. Another useful feature in conjunction with transparent hatches are shades and bug screens, which are integrated in more expensive models or can be retrofitted without too much trouble later.

## ➢ SAIL CONTROL LINES TO COCKPIT ≺

If you are the least bit serious about sailing big on a small sailboat, an arrangement for leading halyards and other lines back to the cockpit is absolutely essential. The industry has recognized the value of this practice because it makes single-handed operation possible and it is safer when it is blowing hard because the crew doesn't have to leave the cockpit to make some basic adjustments to the sail trim. In case you covet an older boat or one that is not yet equipped accordingly, or if you doubt the value of control lines led back to the cockpit, here are some basic tips.

Suppose the breeze is blowing about 15 knots. You let go of the tiller and climb onto the cabintop to raise the sails. Of course,

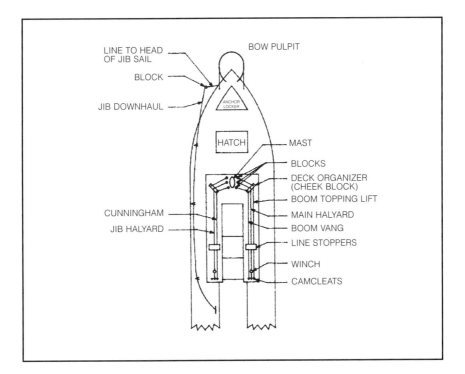

Figure 3-1. Aft-led halyard system: top view

you uncleat the main and jib sheets to permit the sails to luff in the breeze while you are up there, and the tiller is unattended. What happens, however, if the breeze shifts, one of the sheets gets snagged, and a sail fills while you are still up there all alone? What do you do when the boat starts to sail away? And what to do if another vessel approaches? The point is that you usually don't have to put up with such problems if you have a system for leading your halyards and other lines back aft to the cockpit. See Figure 3-1.

Each control line needs a turning block at the mast step. If your boat doesn't have a provision called a mast organizer, you may have to purchase one or bolt the blocks to the cabin roof with backing plates. I have installed six blocks to handle the main and jib halyards, a topping lift, the boom vang, and a cunningham and left one block open for future additions. At about the curvature of the cabintop, I have installed the deck organizers (a set of horizontal check blocks) with three turning blocks angled to enable the halyards to turn the corner and head back toward the cockpit.

The lines are then led aft on both sides of the companionway through rope clutches, which organize and cleat them. On small boats (under 22 feet) cam cleats with fairleads might be used in lieu of rope clutches. If the line is under heavy load, like the main halyard, mount a rope clutch forward of a winch on the cabin top.

With this arrangement all you need to do is remove the sailties, hoist the sails from the cockpit, and you are on your way. Upon returning, the procedure is reversed, you uncleat the halyards and let the sails drop. Even if you must assist the mainsail by pulling on it from the cockpit, it is still a whole lot easier than climbing up on the cabintop.

The standard working jib is a smaller and lighter sail than the main and sometimes it really hesitates to drop to the deck when the jib halyard is uncleated. The force of gravity has less effect on this sail and the breeze has a tendency to keep it up the headstay, flapping in the wind. To avoid having to leave the cockpit and getting white knuckles trying to take down the jib, you can install a downhaul device that will enable you to bring the jib to the deck from the cockpit.

## ➢ JIB DOWNHAULS ➤

It's a bit of an anachronism but a practical one that improves comfort and safety for singlehanded sailing because it eliminates the need to go forward to douse the headsail. Besides, a jib downhaul is simple and inexpensive to install. Of course, roller-furling systems that have become ubiquitous today don't need a downhaul, so this tip is for purists who shun furling mechanisms or owners of older boats. The system requires a small block with a sheave that will handle a ¼" line, enough of the line to ride up the head-

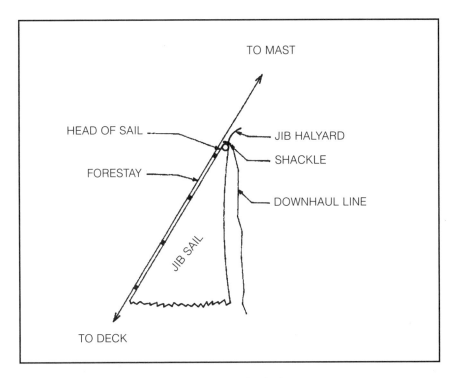

Figure 3-2. A typical jib downhaul system

stay with the jib and extend back to the cockpit, and perhaps some
fairleads and a small cleat. Figure 3-2 shows how it is set up.

One end of the ¼" line has a shackle fixed to it that is fastened
around the halyard above the head of the sail. The other end of the
line (the "bitter end") is run through a block attached to the bow pulpit and then through the lifeline stanchions. The line is then routed
back to the cockpit and a small cleat mounted in a convenient place.
If you don't like the idea of routing the downhaul line through the
lifeline stanchion bases, you can attach two or three bulls-eye fairleads on the deck and run it through them to get the line back to the
cockpit. When installed, the system is very easy to use. All you do is
uncleat the jib halyard from the aft-led system and then pull on the
jib downhaul. When you do, the jib will fall politely to the foredeck.

## ➤ HEADSAIL ROLLER FURLING SYSTEMS ◄

Jib furling systems used to be a pain and have had a reputation of being unreliable. One veteran sailor coined the term "roller failing." But the tireless work of engineers at companies like Harken, Profurl, Facnor and others has produced technology that has made roller-furling headsails an integral part of cruising. They make it easy to set and strike a foresail and they allow the crew to adjust the headsail's size without changing it, so an argument can be made that the installation of a 1,000-dollar furling system might save you from buying a new jib or genoa.

I don't want to get into a long description of these systems— you can do more in-depth research about them online or at any West Marine store. Essentially, a headsail furler/reefer consists of a drum that attaches to the stemhead fitting, a long extrusion or foil for the jib luff, and a swivel between the foil and the top of the headstay. A furling line is led back from the drum to the cockpit where it is cleated. The line is wound up on the drum when the sail is unfurled (by simply uncleating it and trimming the jib sheets so the wind fills the sail and unwinds it completely) and is pulled to furl the sail up.

Furling systems operate on the same principle as old-fashioned, spring-loaded window shades. Just as you pull on the cord to raise the window shade, you pull on the jib sheet to unfurl the sail, and you release it to let it wind up around itself. And like the old fashioned window shades, you can expose as much or as little of it as you desire. Newer furling systems use endless furling lines and split drums that can be removed easily without unhooking the forestay.

If you are at all unsure about your ability to install one of the systems, get a professional to do it for you. These systems are too costly to make mistakes with.

## ➢ ROPE CLUTCHES ≺

We have previously mentioned these devices in our discussion of
the aft-led halyard system. On trailerable sailboats they are typically used for this purpose only. One piece of advice—they come
in sizes to accommodate one, two or three lines and you should
buy the size you are most likely to grow into. Doing so will save
you a little money and, more importantly, will make your deck
look neater than two or three single-sheet stoppers mounted side
by side.

## ➢ DECK LIGHTS ≺

Running lights and a masthead light are not all that is needed for
a trailerable sailboat that's supposed to sail big. Sure, you can get
by fine with just these lights. However, if you are dedicated to sailing big at night, you need a deck light mounted on the mast or the
underside of the spreaders. A deck light is fitted to the mast well
below the steaming or masthead light, and is designed to illuminate the foredeck area so you can move about safely after the sun
goes down. In addition, the more of your boat you can illuminate
until the traffic settles down for the evening, the less likely it is
that someone will run into you. The budget solution for this appli-
cation is a good headlamp with LED lights that will not sap the
battery when used for a couple of hours.

## ➢ THE COCKPIT ≺

Cockpits can be wonderfully pleasant or hellishly awful places in
which to spend your time on a sailboat. That's why I have been baf-
fled about how much time and money people spend making the cabins liveable, and how little thought goes into making the cockpit

more comfortable. They seem to believe that before they are entitled to enjoy a relaxed evening in the cabin, they must somehow earn it by suffering all day in a rude and crude cockpit. I couldn't disagree more. The cockpit is the place from where skipper and crew operate the boat, therefore it has to be functional and practical.

One nuisance are the loose tails of sheets and control lines floating around on the cockpit sole, for two reasons: They get tangled up with your feet and they cause nasty slips and falls when the boat heels and they are stepped on. The solution is simple and effective: Install sheet bags made from mesh and held in place by either suction caps or hook-and-loop fabric. If you have winch handles, make sure they live in separate pockets when not in use and don't wait until you've lost one.

However, when the hook is down or the dock is alongside, it is also a space for relaxing and reading, cooking, or entertaining. On trailerable sailboats, cockpits are usually about six or seven feet long and defined by *cockpit seats*, the *sole* (floor), and the *coamings*. Technically, the coamings are the raised sides of the cockpit, doubling as backrests. The higher they are, the more comfortable and the safer the cockpit will be. The coamings should be angled outboard somewhat so you won't be sitting bolt upright when leaning back, or getting pitched down when the boat is heeled over. On well-designed boats it takes a pronounced step to get over the coamings to walk forward on the side deck.

Cockpit seats should be wide enough to accommodate an adult's rear-end, and high enough from the sole so your knees are not at your chin when sitting down. On the Rhodes 22, the cockpit seats have open fronts, which makes it possible to tuck the feet under and sit comfortably like on a chair. The sole of the cockpit should be wide enough to move around with relative ease and offer enough space to accommodate individuals with size 12 or 13 shoes. Even if you have small feet you still benefit from a good-size cockpit sole because it makes it easier to walk safely and for adults to pass each other.

Assuming the coamings are adequately high and angled, the seats are wide and high enough, and the sole is sufficiently wide, let's look at how to make the cockpit as big as possible. Probably the easiest and quickest change with immediate impact on comfort is adding thick cockpit cushions for the seats and the coamings. But take care to buy cushions that are heavy if you intend to use them under way so they won't be blown overboard, and make sure that they can handle moisture, so they won't fall prey to mildew. Doing it right means to spend some real money.

One additional recommendation for equipping the cockpit for sailing "big," is to purchase and install a bimini top. Biminis are to a sailboat cockpit what air-conditioning is to a home in places where summer heat exceeds 100 degrees. A bimini consists of a large cloth cover made of canvas or vinyl that is fitted over an aluminum frame, which is mounted to the deck or cockpit coamings. The frame is bolted to the boat and tie-downs attach the bimini frame to the lifeline stanchions and the sternrail or to dedicated fittings. When not in use, the bimini folds down over the cabintop. Biminis won't withstand the

Etap 21. A table is essential for "sailing big,"
because it quickly transforms the cockpit into a dining room.

force of a severe blow or keep out rain that's driven at an angle, but under normal conditions they provide shade from the hot, harmful ultraviolet rays of the sun, retard dewfall at night, and transform the cockpit from a place where one endures the elements to one where one actually enjoys sailing and lounging. Investing into a sturdy bimini with high-quality canvas broadens the enjoyment of your trailerable sailboat, and is a significant contribution to sailing big.

A popular option, of course, is turning the cockpit into the dining area on mild summer nights (provided the bugs are not an aggressive nuisance). The options are foldable tables that resemble camping furniture or the more sturdy and nautical pedestal tables that plug into a base on the cockpit floor and can be disassembled in a flash. Manufacturers often provide the latter as an option. When it's time to get going again, unlock the quick release, extract the leg, separate the tabletop and stow the whole thing neatly under a cockpit seat. Companies like Todd (www.toddusa.com) or Garelick (www.garelick.com) sell after-market cockpit tables in many shapes and sizes.

### ➢ SUMMARY ≺

In this discussion of the deck and cockpit arrangements of trailerable sailboats, much has been omitted. I have tried to focus on the layouts and systems that relate to sailing big. Whether we like it or not, people will form opinions about sailboats and their owners based on appearance, and the first thing they see is the outside of the boat. Luckily, there is a correlation between the appearance and the ability of sailing big on a trailerable sailboat.

In Chapter 4 we will turn our attention to the interior space because, below deck, the possibilities to make improvements are as numerous as they are above. Once again, our focus will be on comfort and sailing big.

# 4

# *Belowdecks*

## ➢ INTRODUCTION ≺

Some calculation reveals a stunning fact: The space available in a minivan is roughly the same as in a trailerable sailboat. Cars, like boats are equipped ready to "drive away," for a base price to get you from Point A to Point B. If you desire real comfort, however, you will have to pay for a long list of options. It's the same with sailboats; they too are sold in a basic configuration at a base price, which often doesn't even include sails and destination charges and some other vital stuff. If you want to sail away in comfort, start going down the list of options and break out the checkbook. Start small and start slow, there's always more to add. Think about weight and how much each addition to the cabin will impact displacement, thus affecting the boat's sailing ability.

Three things affect the interior volume of any sailboat: beam, length of the cockpit and general hull shape. If the beam is defined as maximum width, the question is how quickly it narrows when moving forward or going aft. Generally speaking, a cockpit can be made larger only by reducing the size of the cabin, and vice versa. It might be prudent to sacrifice a little cockpit space on a boat to gain some additional room in the cabin. Don't give up too much, however. If you don't have a cockpit large enough to seat four adults in comfort, you can forget entertaining or bringing squirmy

if the cockpit will not accommodate four seated
..e a six-foot adult won't be able to stretch out, and
. uttle siesta, which would drastically diminish the cock-
appeal. The trend, one that started in France, is to maximize
interior space by carrying beam as far aft as possible, just check the
line drawings of the accommodation plans of any cruisable sailboat
designed within the recent past. But most importantly your boat
must suit you personally and fit into your plans.

## ➢ VENTILATION ➣

Okay, there you are on a hot, humid summer evening and absolutely
no air moving. Every drink you place on any surface immediately
leaves a pool of water and every piece of paper you touch sticks to
your skin. How do you keep cool? A good answer to this question
requires thought and research. Fiberglass, as practical as it is as a
building material for production boats, transmits sound and temperature much more than wood. In full sun, fiberglass warms quickly
and the heat is transmitted into the cabin in a very short time. The
most logical solution is to create as much airflow as possible, which
is achieved by good ventilation, both active and passive. Creature
comforts aside, another important benefit of circulating a lot of air
through the boat is making the interior less susceptible to mold and
mildew growth when the vessel is not in use.

### Passive ventilation

- Open hatches and the pop-top, if your boat has one.
- Install cowl, mushroom or clamshell vents that provide a
  path for air to enter and leave the interior.
- Set up a self-supporting Windscoop, an intelligent, simple
  device that resembles a mini-spinnaker. It captures moving
  air and funnels it down through the hatch into the cabin.
  This works really well—so well, in fact, that even the

slightest breeze will have a profound cooling effect on the cabin interior.

- Lewmar offers vents for their hatches to let air into the cabin when they are closed.

### Active Ventilation

- The easiest to install is an electric fan. The secret here is to find an efficient model that minimizes battery drain, yet generates good airflow while oscillating. There is a wide variety of fans available from marine supply stores and catalogs. I suggest you get a fan designed for marine use rather than a cheap unit from a discount store. One suggestion is to position the fan near the open companionway and let it blow forward toward the bow compartment's open deck hatch.

- Install so-called solar vents that have an integrated fan that's operated with electric power from a battery and solar cells on the outside. These gadgets operate around the clock and also help keep the interior dry when the boat is in dry storage.

- The third option represents true extravagance. I'm talking about onboard air-conditioning, the height of luxury. Small boat air conditioners come in either a portable or permanent (self-contained) variety. I don't recommend either one, because I would continually worry about the problem of condensation. Also, other than the dramatic initial cost factor ($1,000 and up), one must consider the fact that these units only work on small boats when plugged into shore power. I prefer a low-tech solution with a basic battery-powered cabin fan and a Windscoop. That's simple and will work while underway.

### Screens and Shades

There will be times when you are going to be anchored with the covered pop-top up and there will be absolutely no breeze blowing anywhere—most certainly not in your sailboat cabin. If it's summertime and you are anchored for the evening, you can count on being visited by mosquitoes or the infamous "no-see-ums." As discussed earlier, hatches with integrated or retrofitted screens remedy this problem quite effectively.

To keep sun out and create a modicum of privacy (e.g. in a separate head compartment), look for hatches with integrated shades. Lewmar (www.lewmar.com) and Oceanair (http://uk.oceanair.co.uk) make integrated roller shade/screen combos that can be retrofitted.

On really rare occasions, all efforts to cool off may fail. If this happens I have a sure-fire recipe that's guaranteed to work: Take off your clothes, throw a safety line overboard that's tied to a strong point on your boat, and jump right in!

### ➤ HEADROOM ◄

You may not have given this idea much thought, but it sure helps to be able to sit belowdecks and hold your head up. On most trailerable sailboats in the 22- to 26-foot range, this will not be a problem if you are sitting in or near the center of the boat's cabin. If you are as tall or taller than I am, you know how frustrating it can be to find yourself sitting somewhere with a ceiling so low that you either must slouch down or not raise your head.

On a sailboat with a traditional trunk cabin you will find that the headroom is limited when one leans back while seated on the settees. Given the design limitations on trailerable sailboats, there isn't much you can do about this fact. I simply encourage you to sit in several parts of a cabin to make certain you can live with the available headroom. This issue disappears on boats with cabin tops that are carried out to the gunwales.

Relief comes on boats with pop tops, which once were popular on camper vans before RVs reached the size of busses. Pop tops on the Catalina 22 or the Rhodes 22 are operated with simple hinge mechanisms raising the cabin tops and with it the headroom.

## ➤ FOOTROOM ◄

This is an area that most first-time sailboat buyers usually don't give a lot of thought. I once owned a 19-foot compact cruiser with a centerboard trunk that intruded into the cabin and split the sole in half. I had to sit slew-footed when I was belowdecks. It was miserable. If you are considering a trailerable boat with below-deck accommodations I encourage you to check out the footroom in the cabin. As a simple rule, boats that have retractable keels or centerboards will have a mechanism somewhere amidships to hoist and lower the appendage, which most likely will reduce the space on the cabin sole.

## ➤ COURTESY LIGHTING ◄

With a production model of a trailerable sailboat, you shouldn't have high expectations about lighting in the cabin area. It's not much of a problem during the daylight hours, particularly if you have a pop-top with your boat, but that's not much help at night. Luckily there are hundreds of possibilities to retrofit any boat with utility lighting or courtesy lights from any marine supply store. Especially the new energy-efficient LED lights (some of them rated at more than 200,000 hours of use) work well with a small boat's extremely limited power. The available variety of lamp styles is pretty good—from the really nautical to the ultra-modern. You can buy stick-up fluorescent lights, incandescent dome lights or flush-mount LED lamps. Or you go entirely retro and opt for salty-looking lamps fueled by oil, which operate independently from the boat's batteries, but are not bright enough for reading. Another valuable suggestion derived from years of experience: Two areas that need a good light if they are to be of any use at night are galley and head.

## ➤ STORAGE ◄

Suppose you are going on a weekend cruise possibly with your spouse and one or two kids. It won't be difficult to bring everything you need on the boat—clothes and food, fuel for cooking, pots, pans, dishes and cups, foul weather gear, ice, games for the children, blankets, towels, etc. The fun part is stowing everything so it is safe and easily accessible. There is nothing more frustrating or upsetting than discovering that all of the seats and berths are covered with clothes, towels, or bags of food. Furthermore, if you leave this stuff sitting around while you are sailing, it will slide, shift or fly around and eventually it will all be a tangled mess on the cabin sole.

On most modern trailerable sailboats storage is built into the berths in the saloon and the forecabin, into the galley and as a lazarette into the space under the cockpit seats. Over time you will find ways to organize your boat better as you personalize the cabin. While visiting other boats, I have seen the ingenuity people use to modify the interior to create additional storage space, eg. with canvas hanging lockers, galley organizers, collapsible plastic crates, utility mesh bags, gear hammocks and the like.

While having storage space is important, intelligent usage of that space is equally significant. Here a bit of backpacking or camping experience is helpful because these activities require packing discipline. You bring what you need, you know how to stow it and you know where to find it when you need it. Separate your gear by function and use stuff sacks or small containers, if possible transparent or labeled. Don't mix canned foods with clothes, or board games with emergency equipment such as flashlights, flares or the medical kit. If it has to stay dry, use waterproof sea bags. They are tough, come in different colors (including transparent) and sizes and can be folded up small when not in use. Check out camping and kayak outfitters since they carry many practical items for this purpose. It's also a good idea to carry some plastic bags onboard to keep wet bathing suits and clothes separated from things that you don't want to get wet.

As I mentioned previously, most trailerable sailboats will have storage compartments molded in under most, if not all, of the seats and berths. These offer fairly decent amounts of storage space. In addition, the boats usually provide some storage space associated with the galley. If you use that space and do a little creative addition of storage space yourself, you will be able to sail just as big as the guys on the 40-footers. Rest assured, they have a storage problem too.

## ➤ TOILETS ➤

On small trailerable sailboats the bathroom or head usually consists of a portable chemical toilet (porta-potti), and it is usually optional on a production boat. It is simple and functional, and environmentally sound because it doesn't discharge any human waste overboard. On the other hand it's also very basic; even the best maintained porta-potti smells somewhat, which is noticeable in the cabin especially when there is no dedicated, closed-off space for it. Besides, the first mate might demand an enclosed head if she is to become a regular participant in longer outings. That's why several eminently trailerable and very capable little cruisers above 24 feet in length have a toilet compartment that's closed off from the cabin and can be equipped with a marine toilet and a separate holding tank.

But as much as manufacturers strive to offer it as an option where technically and practically feasible, it still has to be a compromise on a trailerable boat, one that affords a modicum of privacy, but little elbowroom. The drawback of a marine sanitation system is its complexity with hoses, valves, seacocks and a holding tank, which can be discharged overboard where legal or emptied at a marine pump-out station. At the very least, a marine sanitation system requires a knowledgeable hand for proper installation. At the same time it is also another system that can fail and will, eventually. Don't take a manufacturer's word for it, just ask a seasoned cruiser, how often they had to replace, or worse, rebuild the head.

Let's focus on portable heads since they are most likely what you will end up with. These usually come in two parts—a freshwater tank with about a three-gallon capacity (top), and a holding tank (bottom), which contains the waste and the cleaner/deodorant to treat the waste. As mentioned earlier, porta-pottis are simple and compact, which means they can live under the V-berth or under the companionway steps and don't smell too bad as long as they are clean and properly maintained. They are also very easy to operate, rarely ever clog and hold waste in a separate holding tank, which is portable and makes them environmentally correct. But they are not fun to empty, because someone has to drag the detachable holding tank to a toilet and discharge it there.

Once that's done you should clean the head with one of the numerous bowl cleaners and holding tank treatments offered by your friendly marine supply store or by pouring a little vinegar water in the holding tank. Take this job very seriously—portable heads should be emptied and cleaned right after returning from a sail, no exceptions—it will save you from trouble and from enduring a smelly cabin, especially in hot weather.

The best advice I can give you is not to buy a cheap, poorly constructed porta-potti. Approximately $150 will get you a "deluxe" model with a five-gallon holding tank, which should suffice for a weekend trip.

## ➤ GALLEY ◄

Although sailboat galleys are not what you would normally associate with the word "kitchen," they *should* provide all of the equipment and devices necessary for efficient meal preparation. There are a number of different arrangements for setting up a galley in a small sailboat and none of them involve lots of counter space. With space being limited, many manufacturers were searching for

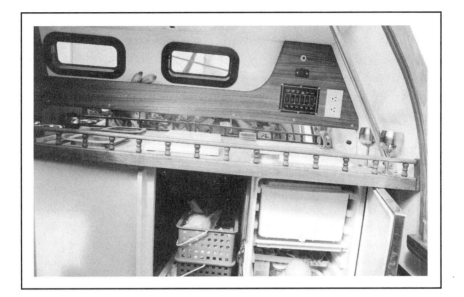

Rhodes 22. Homey, compact and functional,
the galley is the heart of every ship. Even if it is only 22 feet long.

a practical compromise, which means that the galley often doubles
as a navigation desk or that the galley modules are moveable. This
assumes that you won't be whipping up a four-course meal when
under way and that you can wait to add another chapter to your
small-boat cruising memoir until after dinner when the boat's
docked or swinging from a hook.

### Sinks

Above all, galley sinks need to be deep. Sailboat manufacturers
can provide you with sinks that are really functional, or they can
provide tiny little bowl-shaped things that are very shallow and
will slosh the water out with the slightest heel to the boat. Party
boats (and catamarans) will have shiny but shallow sinks, which
work fine at rest, but are not so practical for under way. Serious
blue-water boats can be recognized by, among other things, a pair

of sinks with steep walls (no bowls) more than six inches deep. If you are not satisfied with the original sink on your boat, you can always try and install an after-market product that fits the original's cutout.

A sink is not very functional if it is too shallow to hold any utensils or not wide enough to get a small pot down in it for washing, but the reality on small boats is cramped and you most likely won't be able to install a much larger model than what's already there. Personally I prefer stainless steel sinks over plastic or fiberglass because it doesn't stain and scratch.

In an ideal world, there should be some counter space associated with the sink. Don't expect much surface area, but make certain there is some available to put objects down. In case there is none, you have to get creative and add some temporary space, either by using a large cutting board or in a real pinch you might have to commandeer part of a settee.

### Fresh Water

Most trailerable sailboats in our size range will be delivered with a manual water pump and a small, sometimes portable fresh-water tank. These manual pumps work pretty well, requiring somewhere between 45 and 55 strokes to deliver a gallon of water. So you can see that it doesn't take much work to get a glass of fresh water, or enough to make a cup of coffee.

If you have to replace or refit this item, use a model that has a swiveling spout and a handle that has a back-and-forth action, rather than up-and-down. Two other advantages of those rocker pump faucets are their simplicity, which makes them easy to maintain and their versatility, handling both fresh and saltwater. Some manufacturers of trailerable cruising boats might offer the option of pressure water dispensed by electrical pumps, but frankly, on a boat of 26 feet or less that's a weighty luxury one probably can forego.

A few thoughts about storing water are in order. The holding tanks can be either rigid (when built in) or soft and collapsible (when portable). Rigid tanks are usually more difficult to clean and maintain, while the collapsible kind can be carried off the boat and filled with fresh water from your home. This last point is a real plus because as you probably know, the fresh water found around most lakesides or coastal marinas has a peculiar taste to it. You may also notice a little plastic taste in your fresh water. If so, a small amount of vinegar water usually helps take the plastic edge out of the taste.

If you are going on a cruise, you have to calculate with at least one gallon of water per person a day, so that can be a real limitation on a small boat. The remedy can be as simple as adding some jerry jugs, which need to be stowed near the center of pitch and gravity (in the middle of the boat and near the water line, if possible), so they least impede performance. Or if it's in the budget, you can bring a watermaker, which turns seawater into fresh water. These portable manual units are marvels of technology that use the principle of reverse osmosis like their powered larger siblings. But they are not cheap and still require elbow grease for continuous pumping to produce a gallon of potable water per hour.

### Stoves

You can get stoves with one or two burners, either flush-mounted or gimbaled, the latter being a necessity if any cooking is to happen while under way. You can buy stoves that are fueled by pressurized or non-pressurized alcohol, or butane and there are other combinations as well. On a small boat, you probably need to be happy with a two-burner stove. Often, the production model of a trailerable sailboat will come with a provision for a flush-mounted, non-pressurized alcohol stove. While they are okay, I prefer butane because it is instantly hot and cooks in a shorter time.

Examine carefully the location of the stove with one thought in mind: Is there anything immediately above or near the stove that will easily catch fire in case of an accident such as a flare-up when lighting the stove, or because of spilled oil, etc? Look the area over carefully and make certain you can cook safely in that location. Something that can be seen on small race boats that do multi-day coastal races or even transoceanic races (e.g. California to Hawaii) are one-burner gimbaled stoves either used in the cockpit or on a special mount in the companionway. Since gourmet meals are not at the top of the checklist on most racing boats, these stoves suffice for simple fare or heating water for coffee and a bag of the yummy freeze-dried stuff.

### Barbecues

Before you jump to conclusions about the rationale of barbecuing on small boats, let me elaborate a little on the benefits of grills mounted on the sternrail. Barbecuing produces flavorful food (steaks, chicken, or that fresh fish you caught earlier in the day) and it expands the galley into the cockpit, which is quite clever on a small boat.

Once, when I had been sailing with two other boats all day, the three of us anchored at Redfish Point in Florida for the evening. After about an hour at anchor, and just as the sun was dipping behind the horizon, the three boats rafted up and the skipper of one of the other boats took charge of the dinner's main course, barbecuing some New York strip steaks. He also wrapped some vegetables in aluminum foil and threw them on the grill. When it was time to eat, he passed out the steaks and vegetables and we sat there under the evening sky, having one of the most delicious meals I can remember.

A few quick pointers for boat barbecues: They come either as kettles with a dome lid or in rectangular versions. Good models are made of marine grade stainless steel to resist corrosion and discoloration. Use gas-powered grills with a piezo igniter since charcoal is a pain and a hazard to store properly on a small boat. Compare BTU ratings for heat output and don't skimp on accessories, because they add a lot of versatility to this device: a good rail mount for safe attachment, a dockstand for on-shore use, radiant burner plates for cooking stews, or a separate grill for smaller items such as vegetables.

Use a canvas cover to protect the unit and don't forget to bring an extra canister of fuel. With a little practice you'll be able to emulate the pros and barbecue while you are riding a gentle breeze on a beam reach. And that is a fine example for sailing big.

### Refrigeration

Let's face it, barbecues are nice, but I don't know any sailor worth his salt who thinks a barbecue is more important than a cooler. On small boats, refrigeration will most likely come in the form of a portable cooler that's large enough to hold a weekend's worth of perishable foods and beer. These coolers can be cheap and are simple to add to a boat's gear and come in many sizes. Some of them even resemble carry-on luggage with wheels and pull-out handle.

First, there is the question of the size of the cooler: Is it large enough to hold any meaningful amount of ice and food or drinks? Remember, you are probably going to have a block of ice in there and still need room for food and drinks.

Second, does it have insulated sides or is it simply a fiberglass container? Once the ice is gone, all the cold is gone and what good is that? Therefore the chest should have sides that are thick enough to hold some insulation. A good practice perfected by thrifty cruisers is partitioning the icebox by inserting insulating pads and Styrofoam boards between the ice and the food, so both last longer.

Third, the chest should open from the top (and almost all do) because cold air is heavier and remains in the bottom so you will lose less of that precious commodity if the lid is on top.

The rule of thumb is to bring the biggest cooler that can safely fit into its allotted space on the boat. Sometimes a cooler doubles as the bottom step of the companionway, which is smart, because there it's out of the way, yet easily accessible from the cockpit and the cabin.

If the boat has a built-in icebox, resist the temptation to convert it into a reefer/freezer because it adds more gear, more weight and more worries. Compressor, evaporator, hoses, connectors, fittings, insulation and (ozone-friendly) coolant are only the beginning of the story. The real issue is generating the power to run it when you are under way.

Because good refrigeration is the key to enjoyable cruising, you might want to look into coolers that are used by professional fishermen, but be prepared for sticker shock: A box with a capacity of 200 quarts can cost you more than $500, but you get what you pay for: It has 1½-inch insulation, it's super rugged and it's watertight when the lid is latched down, so it floats. Indeed, there are stories about offshore fishermen who clung to a floating cooler until rescue arrived after their vessel had gone down.

## ➤ DINETTE ≺

Okay, you have prepared a repast in your galley and now you and your company are ready to sit down for dinner. The pop-top is raised, the Windscoop is up, and there is a gentle breeze moving through the cabin. A bottle of chilled wine has emerged from the cooler, you uncork it and put on your favorite tune just for the occasion.

Obviously, you shouldn't expect Grandmother's 12-foot dining table on a sailboat of this size, but you should have a table that seats three or four persons in relative comfort as they enjoy culinary delights, either above or below decks.

Space is a scarce commodity on a small sailboat, so designers often had to assign multiple uses to several areas of the boat, e.g. a nav table that converts into a galley or a dinette that converts into a single or double berth. Often, neither purpose was served to satisfaction, but the learning curve has gotten flatter and in many instances, the compromises are quite acceptable.

The saloon tables on most trailerable sailboats can actually be used for sitting down and enjoying a meal, even in relative comfort. Nevertheless, there are a number of things you should consider when choosing a boat.

### Cabin Table

You need a dining table with enough surface area to set the table properly. Although this may be obvious to you, it isn't always as obvious to the sailboat manufacturers. The trouble with tables is that they need to be out of the way when no meal is served to save space, therefore small cruising boats almost always have saloon tables that fold up, down, or away. Sometimes if the table folds down from the forward bulkhead it's long and narrow, resembling an ironing board. If that's the case and you like everything else about the vessel, don't despair. Any reasonably talented carpenter, or a dedicated home worker with the proper tools can turn a fold-down table into a fold-down-and-fold-out table by adding a leaf on hinges to increase the surface if necessary.

If the dinette hooks into a bulkhead on one end and is supported by a single leg that inserts into a hole in the cabin sole on the other end, check and see if it is stable. Go to the end of the table nearest the leg and press down on a corner. If the table rocks, look and see if there is a way to keep it from doing so. It was a problem on my Catalina 22, and it can be on larger boats, but again some basic carpentry can solve the issue. One practical thought: Make sure that whatever mechanism is devised and installed, it must be foolproof to operate, especially in the dark. Seasoned cruisers will agree. If the table can migrate to the cockpit for al-fresco dining, all the better (see previous chapter).

### Knee Room and Backrests

Sit down at the table and make certain that it is sufficiently high for an adult to get the knees under it. If you are not tall and your knees go easily under the table, stop and think about guests you may have onboard. Will they be able to get their knees under the table, too? Spend five minutes to check it out and fix it, if necessary. It'll make life aboard, especially at dinnertime, much more pleasant. If you have small kids, don't worry. A cushie booster or an additional cockpit cushion will elevate them to the proper height.

Another matter of comfort is the depth of the settee and the backrest behind it (if there is any at all). What's comfortable to lounge or sleep on, is probably less so for dining. Modern boats often have fold-down backrests that provide a modicum of support when sitting upright at the table. Older ones that don't have this feature require a bit of improvising with cushions to spruce up back support. Again, try it out before you cast off and make sure you have a solution worked out before you go.

### Dinner Lighting

Just a brief note about lighting. It helps to be able to see what's for dinner. In the cockpit that's no problem: A petroleum or oil lamp strung up on the boom above the cockpit table will do the job and score high in the mood department. Down below, the courtesy reading lights aren't in the right spot and rarely are bright enough to do justice to the cause. It might be necessary to install a separate dome light, and it's up to an owner's interior decoration skills to choose the right one. Fluorescent lights are cheap and relatively energy-efficient, but spread the charm of a waiting room at the hospital. Lights with incandescent bulbs provide a warmer glow, but draw more power and need more maintenance. Perhaps it's time to check out the low-power and low-maintenance LED technology? Or maybe going retro is your choice: If the cabin is well vented, a small brass oil lamp on the bulkhead might be all you need. It looks salty and won't sap the battery when you're swinging on the hook.

## ➢ WINDOW CURTAINS ≺

Window curtains for the cabin give the interior a finished, almost homey look, but on small boats they are usually a pricey option.

One way to avoid it is to wait for the right moment to ask the first mate if there's interest in an off-season project that does not require sanding, painting or varnishing. Knowing a little bit of the role assignments in real life, I surmise that the question (or is it a strong suggestion?) about new, different or nicer curtains might often come from the first mate. It doesn't matter who's in charge of such a project, but the consensus among first mates and connoisseurs is that curtains belong on a boat that must offer some comfort and a smidgen of privacy. As an added benefit, curtains made of a light fabric also help keep the cabin cooler. If there is no sewing machine with a qualified and willing operator to be found in the household, there are after-market kits available, from metal rods to hook-and-loop stick-ups that will serve the purpose in a pinch and permit you to make your own curtains and install them yourself.

## ➢ PRIVACY CURTAINS ≺

Privacy curtains are most simple and cost-effective devices that close off the V-berth area and/or the head from the rest of the cabin. If you're used to the uncomplicated and carefree arrangements on stripped-down race boats, you will probably have experienced the token privacy of a head behind a curtain. On a small cruising boat installing a set of curtains is often the only way to create a private space. Plus they have other advantages: On my Catalina 22, Robert, my then 18-year-old son would spend the night on the boat after a date with his girlfriend. Because he is a late sleeper, he would crawl into the V-berth and close the privacy curtains to keep out the morning sun, if necessary until 11:00 o'clock.

If the sailboat you want to buy doesn't have these privacy curtains, I would recommend that you install them. It's easy and inexpensive, and you'll be glad you did, either for your crew or guests who might like some privacy or for yourself on those mornings when you'd like to stay in bed for a little while longer.

## ➢ BERTHS ➢

You may be very different from me, but after a good, hard day of sailing I usually retire quite early and, as a result, arise almost with the sun in the morning. The reason is really simple—I have a comfortable berth to sleep on and I rest well. But that wasn't always the case. From personal experience, I know there's absolutely nothing worse than to have to squeeze into one of those coffin-like quarterberths and try to sleep. The bunk on a Navy destroyer I served on was more comfortable. I once spent five consecutive nights sleeping in one of those tiny quarterberths and was exhausted every morning.

First look at the thickness of the cushions on all of the berths. Cushions should at least be three inches thick, but four inches are desirable. Next check the width of the berths. I have found that you need about 30 inches for one person and around 60+ inches for two people. If it is a single berth, it will be no fun if one shoulder hangs off the side. If the manufacturer claims that the dinette converts into a double berth, find out if they mean a double for two small children, an adult and one child, or two adults. Examine the V-berth that gets narrower toward the bow of the boat and see if there's enough shoulder room for two adults and if there is enough foot room forward.

Several boats (like the MacGregor 26 or the Hunter 25) have astonishingly spacious berths under the cockpit, thanks to a design trick that turned these berths sideways.

I only know one way to make certain that a berth is of sufficient length, and that is to lie down on it in all three positions—back, side, and stomach. If you are six feet tall and you sleep on your stomach, your toes are going to extend another two to three inches beyond your normal six-foot frame. Even on small boats berths that should accommodate adults are around 6 feet 4 inches long.

When checking out a quarterberth that extends under the cockpit seats, make certain that there is enough vertical clearance

Hunter 25. The aft double berth is tucked away under the cockpit floor,
behind the companionway steps and a portable cooler.

for you to raise your knees slightly and turn over. If you can't, you
will have to stay in one position all night, and that's agony.

Another important factor aside from the thickness of the
mattress is its material and breathability. It doesn't have to an expensive inner spring mattress with German micro coils, latex
cushioning and what not. But it certainly helps if the mattress
properly supports shoulders and hips and if it breathes to prevent
excessive sweating and to reduce the risk of mildew growth.
Putting down a flexible grid of slats as suspension sometimes is
all you need to create separation between the bunk and the mattress. One option is the German Froli Sleep System represented
in the U.S. by Nickle Atlantic (www.nickleatlantic.com). It won't
be cheap, but a good night's rest might be worth it.

## ➤ SUMMARY ≺

Let me encourage you to think of the cabin on your trailerable sailboat as your home on the high seas: You have a "kitchen," a "living room" or "den," a "bathroom," and "bedrooms." Admittedly, these areas are somewhat downsized on a trailerable sailboat, but they are, nevertheless, real definable spaces. If you are at all like me, you want your home to be as comfortable as possible. You will probably want the same for your sailboat. Since hardly any boat comes perfectly equipped from the factory, use your own imagination, ingenuity and hopefully these tips that were derived through experience to turn the living space of your boat into an environment that's perfect for you and the way you use your vessel.

# 5

# *The Challenges*

*There is no substitute for knowing your ship, its capabilities, and your own. There is no substitute for preplanning and practice, both for yourself and your crew. And there is no substitute for calm, rational action when an emergency arises.*

TONY MEISEL, Nautical Emergencies

## ➤ INTRODUCTION ◄

Now that you have bought a trailerable sailboat, tweaked it, tuned it and fitted it out belowdecks, are you ready to go sailing? The answer is no, not yet, because sailing big does not necessarily equal sailing safely. You should never consider raising your sails until you are certain that you have done everything necessary to make it a safe voyage, no matter how brief or how long.

To go sailing is to accept a challenge. It requires a willingness to deal with the elements: wind, water, currents, tides, and other factors, which can promote or impede a sailboat's progress. It is the sailor's task to prepare the ship so it will stand up to the conditions and safely reach the destination. When successful, this is an exciting and rewarding experience, but it requires careful planning and preparation. Avoiding problems is better than fixing them and as old salts like Des Sleightholme suggest, "Keeping out of trouble is very largely a matter of thinking ahead. A chess mentality. Thinking ahead not only in terms of passage planning but in the small things." In our case, small is beautiful and it is easy to explain why.

A common way of thinking about sailboats implies that bigger means safer, but this is not supported by fact. Countless intrepid voyagers have crossed the Atlantic and Pacific oceans in sailboats well under 20 feet of overall length. Here are a few points that work to the advantage of a small boat.

- Size of sail area: Every sail on a trailerable sailboat is smaller and lighter than the equivalent on a big boat, which means it is easier to handle by a small crew or by the skipper alone.
- Rig size: Smaller sails are supported by shorter and lighter spars, and a defect that might have semi-catastrophic consequences on a large boat, like a broken stay or gooseneck, will be easier to deal with.
- Many trailerable sailboats feature positive flotation, which stems from the closed-cell foam of the sandwich laminate. The Etap, the MacGregor 26 and the Rhodes 22 make this point in their marketing materials.

Compared to a larger boat, a trailerable sailboat has fewer things that can go wrong. Furthermore, problems on a small sailboat tend to stay small and manageable. However, most problems on sailboats have nothing to do with the size of the boat, but are a result of mistakes by skipper or crew, inattention, complacency, faulty judgment or simply a lack of skills. Operator error can be reduced to a minimum by careful thought, advance planning, and practicing of the necessary skills. Anticipation, alertness and risk management are key weapons to avoid emergencies.

### ➤ PHYSICAL AND PERSONAL INJURY ≺

In many respects, a trailerable sailboat is a finely tuned machine and, like on other such machines, things can break or go wrong. Standing rigging can snap, your mast can come down, and the rudder can be sheared off. You can hit another boat, run into a submerged object, or an inattentive boater can crash into you. Even if nothing happens to your boat, people can sustain injuries such as bruises, cuts and abrasions. Don't forget sunburn, which can seriously debilitate crew who don't take proper precautions and as a result can't function, thus impeding the safety of your boat.

The same goes for *mal de mer*, the dreaded seasickness, caused by the motion of the boat. Not everyone is equally susceptible, but those who are affect the way the boat is sailed. Seasickness makes victims extremely uncomfortable beyond committing the lunch to Neptune over the leeward rail and impairs their ability to contribute to the vessel's safe operation. It is your responsibility as the skipper to take reasonable precautions to effectively deal with such situations, if and when they arise. It simply makes good sense to have the right safety equipment on board. Although nobody wants to experience it, there are possibilities for physical damage to boat and/or crew, so planning and prevention will put you a step ahead of the game.

### Hitting or Getting Hit

There is absolutely nothing more embarrassing than running into another boat or object (such as a dock), and there is nothing more frustrating than to have another boat run into yours.

If you choose to participate in competitive sailboat racing, you should expect to sustain a few bumps, bangs, and an occasional crunch from fellow racers. This is particularly true when a large number of boats are jockeying for position at the starting line. If, on the other hand, your sailing will be daysailing or short recreational cruises, your boat's bumps, nicks, and gouges will come primarily as a result of two situations:

- Accidentally hitting another boat or object while leaving or returning to the dock, or
- Another boat trying to do the same thing, and hitting you. Luckily, in most cases damage will usually be minimal.

After sailing a small compact cruiser in discomfort for three years, I reached the decision that it was time to move up to a

Catalina 22, and to begin to enjoy my overnighting and cruising. I trailered the Catalina 22 to my club, the Tuscaloosa Sailing Club, put it in the water, and motored it to my berth. While approaching the slip, I killed the outboard exactly where I did on my smaller and lighter compact cruiser. You can guess the rest. I had failed to compensate for the additional 1,000 pounds of weight of the Catalina 22, and the momentum of the boat carried it right past the dock. If the Commodore and Vice Commodore had not been watching this drama as it unfolded, I would have crashed into the large rocks that guarded the shore. Both helped me fend the boat off, and I narrowly avoided serious damage to the bow of my new sailboat. However, they got a good kick out of the incident, which became the topic of lively discussion for the next several days around the sailing club.

Here is some good, hard-learned advice: First, think. Contemplate leaving or entering the dock area before you actually do. Second, plan. Envision your approach or departure. Consider the traffic and the conditions, wind speed, direction, current, the vessel's weight, whether it's loaded or empty. Third, practice. Learn how to maneuver your boat under many different circumstances and take the time to talk untested crew through every step, so they can become familiar with the processes on your boat. Thought, planning and practice are the three secrets that separate amateurs from professionals.

Hydrodynamic principles preclude sailboats from backing up easily. Aside from external conditions, there are several impediments to making good progress going in reverse, including the shape of the hull when the stern becomes the bow, the location of the keel or centerboard, the position of the rudder and the type and position of the engine (inboard with fixed shaft or Saildrive or an outboard).

These are factors you can't change, at least not when you are in the process of executing the maneuver, so you must honor their idiosyncrasies. For example, if you have a swing keel or centerboard, you can experiment with it at various positions to maximize steering control when backing. My advice is to take your boat out to some uncrowded area and practice backing up to see how the boat handles. Experiment by trying different tactics in different conditions, especially with a strong breeze on the beam, and you will develop a feel for how the boat acts and reacts when going backward.

Find out how the boat steers at different speeds. Logic dictates that the slower you go, the more difficult the boat is to steer, because there is hardly any flow on the foils (rudder and keel) to work with.

If you have a swing keel or centerboard, you will find that steering control is significantly diminished when the keel is completely retracted. That's because the keel serves as the pivot point and also facilitates tracking when going straight. Again, experiment and determine how far the swing keel must be lowered to achieve good steerage. In addition, let the boat coast in different conditions by putting the engine in neutral. Try it in smooth water and in choppy seas, on the bow, on the stern and on the beam. The purpose of this exercise is to know how far the boat's weight will carry the hull after the motor has been turned off.

A golden tip: Don't practice this with a fixed dock, at least not when you are in the beginning stages, but do it with a mooring buoy that has a good pick-up stick. Docking a boat in a marina berth is like putting in golf. If you are too slow, you'll fall short, which means you never had a chance to score. If the wind blows from the dock's direction you may find yourself back out in the channel, trying again.

But if you're too fast, your boat's bow will meet the hard pier quite audibly, and bear the scars to tell the story to those who *weren't* there in person to witness the mishap. Many a crew have suffered cuts, bruises, and even mangled bones by trying to fend off another boat or the dock with their hands and feet. *Never, ever fend off a one- or two-ton boat with any body parts when coming into the dock.* It is easier to repair fiberglass and gelcoat than a broken limb. In other words: Erring on the slow side, while still embarrassing, is a much less dangerous mistake.


### Submerged Objects

A fairly common source of damage is the submerged object. Such objects include logs, stumps, rocks, boulders or sandbars. At slow speeds, such collisions result in scrapes on the boat's keel or hull, or perhaps gouges in the gelcoat. It's a different story if your boat's hull or appendages meet a submerged object of sufficient weight and mass at cruising speed and at the wrong angle or in the wrong spot. A fracture or hole in the hull is no joke, especially when it occurs under the waterline.

If this happens, you need to do two things. First locate the damage, and determine if the vessel takes on water. If that's the case, a good electric bilge pump or a frightened crew member with a bucket might be able to extract the amount of water coming in. If the leak is too big for the available pump capacity, immediately stop the boat and expend your best effort to try and minimize the water ingress by stuffing towels and rags into the compromised area, placing a piece of rubber or vinyl matting over it and bracing a rigid object such as a flat piece of wood against it. Since the fracture was caused by an object that struck the hull from the outside, the brace should help re-close the break and slow the intake of water.

Some extra-cautious skippers might have an emergency kit on board that makes it possible to fix a leak with a dense sponge and a putty that is set off when it comes in contact with water. Another way to slow down water is a collision mat, which can be a piece of heavy vinyl fabric that is pulled over the defective hull area from the outside to slow the leak and buy time for making repairs or calling for help. The external water pressure will push against the sailcloth and form a pretty decent seal. An old jib might serve the same purpose in a pinch. If you do have a reasonable doubt about your ability to return safely to shore, you must still undertake a repair effort and call the local authorities on channel 16 of your VHF radio to notify them of your difficulty and request assistance.

Once you have the area sealed to the best of your ability, try to determine the proximity of the break to the waterline. If it is at or near the waterline, try moving crew weight and supplies to the opposite side and heel until the damaged spot is out of the water. On larger boats, the boom can be used as a lever when the main is doused and the topping lift is attached. To be effective, one or more crew have to shimmy as far outboard as possible to heel the boat. This tactic often works for fixed-keel boats that have run aground and try to come free under their own power.

Keep an eye out for submerged objects and make sure your navigation is up to snuff. That's the best and cheapest preparation to avoid collisions. In general, U.S. waterways are well marked for hazards, as are the majority of inland lakes used regularly by sailboats. The problem of submerged objects will be most common after heavy rains, with floating logs and other debris presenting the greatest hazard. Another option is to learn from the boaters in the Pacific Northwest for whom floating logs are a fact of life. Drought, on the other hand, can lower water levels on lakes and produce shoals that weren't there when you last visited the area.

Many trailerable sailboat owners take advantage of the portability of their boats by taking them to new, distant and inviting venues. Hitching your vessel to your vehicle is one of the true benefits of this style of boating. When you arrive at a new venue, simply ask the locals about new hazards in the area that might not be charted properly or have even escaped the Coast Guard's Notice to Mariners. Most boaters are friendly folks who like to help out with good advice, so chances are they will oblige and tell you what they know about local conditions and, as a result, make your trip safer and more enjoyable.

## ➤ HEAVY WEATHER ≺

To beginners there is nothing more frightening than the thought of being caught in a stiff blow, no matter the boat's size. Wind speed increases dramatically as weather systems approach, accompanied by larger and steeper seas that will knock you and your little craft about. Wind velocity and the size and state of the sea are the primary factors that determine your survival strategy.

Fearing the savage sea does not make you a coward. To the contrary, it might be your best life insurance. After all, you can't practice seamanship and boat handling in 30+ knots of wind like you can practice a tee shot. It takes years of sailing to gain the practice, skills and confidence in heavy weather, and even then, the master mariner must always be respectful of the sea. To get you started the right way, here is some time-tried advice that will help flatten the learning curve and ensure your own safety and that of your crew and your boat.

It's only a start, however, so read up on boat handling and storm tactics in the numerous books that have been published about it. One of them is the *Annapolis Book of Seamanship* by John Rousmaniere, which should be part of your on-board library.

- Weather reports: No matter how good it looks out there, always listen to the weather forecast for your area on the weather channel of your VHF. Check it often because it gets updated every few hours. There are a number of excellent Web sites that provide usable weather information, such as the one that's maintained by the National Weather Service (www.nws.noaa.gov/), which you might want to peruse prior to your trip. It'll take a bit of research to find the sources that work best for your area(s) of interest, but once you have identified them, sign up for Real Simple Syndication (RSS) to automatically receive the latest updates on your computer's desktop.

- Local Knowledge: Asking locals for information about hazards to navigation in an unfamiliar sailing venue is only half the story. Ask about weather phenomena and ways to avoid difficult situations. Professional fishermen too are an excellent source of knowledge since they are always on the water, rain or shine. The trick is getting them to divulge what they know.
- Navigation: Have your waypoints plugged into your GPS and familiarize yourself with the shore and possible places to seek shelter. When the storm starts, you are needed at the helm, not down below fiddling with the GPS and trying to divine where to go next.
- Other preparations: If your boat has a swing keel, you can adjust the angle of the keel (meaning hoisting it part of the way) to maintain maximum control under reduced sail area. Tie down stuff that can go overboard or fly through the cabin and do damage; have the sea anchor ready in case you have to slow down the boat; and most importantly, have all aboard put on Personal Flotation Devices. Pass out motion sickness remedy to anyone of the crew (including yourself) who doesn't have good sea legs.
- Shortening sail: It is wrong to assume a certain wind velocity as the time to reef. When you first think about it is the right time. Much depends on how much wind you, your crew and the boat can handle safely with full sail area. Usually the boat will tell the skipper when it is over-canvassed, by heeling too hard and developing a lot of weather helm (the tendency of the boat rounding up into the wind if the tiller is let go) that can't be tamed sufficiently by adjusting the sail trim. In any case, shorten sail before all hell breaks loose and make sure the rest of the boat is ready, too. It's easier to shake out a reef if the boat wants it than to tie one in when the boat is on its ear. In this situation, a roller furling headsail is very practical since it won't require crew on the foredeck to change to a smaller jib. This situation also

demonstrates why having your sail control lines led back to the cockpit is a smart idea. It's not only for comfort but it increases personal safety as well.

- How much sail to take in? Cruising mainsails, even on small boats, have two reef points. If you have not developed references when to go with the No. 1 or No. 2 reef, start with No 1 and leave the jib as is. If you have a roller-furling jib, start winding it in some. If the weather helm becomes too strong, you've shortened the jib too much. If your boat has adjustable jib leads, it is time to move them forward, because a partially rolled up headsail requires different sheeting angles than a fully deployed jib. Strive to sail with two sails as long as possible, because the boat will be better balanced than under main or jib alone. If the wind continues to build, and the vessel continues to misbehave, you are not out of options, but you won't be able to sail to weather. Dropping the main completely and trying to go with the jib only or striking all sails and running before the wind under bare poles are the next steps.

- Running under bare poles: It's a popular survival tactic that only works with open sea room to leeward. To maintain a semblance of control and keep the boat from careening wildly down the breakers, you might be forced to slow down, either by towing a drogue or a warp, formed by a heavy long line that is attached to the cleats at both sides of the stern to form a bight. One caveat: If surf crashes thunderously on a lee shore straight downwind from your position, running before the wind under bare poles won't help.

- Heaving-to: This is the nautical equivalent of hunkering down and letting the boat maintain position (more or less) by itself. It is an accepted practice if sailing is becoming too tedious and the crew needs rest, but like running before bare poles, it requires sea room. Here's how it's being done: Backwind the jib, meaning sheet it on the windward side (the wrong side). Balance the trim of the mainsail and lash the tiller down to leeward, so the boat makes very slow headway and sideway. The pressure of the wind on the back-filled jib will force the bow of the boat down, away from the wind. Once the bow has fallen off the wind, the main will fill and the tiller lashed to leeward will force the boat back closer to the wind. Then, the main will luff and the back-filled jib will again force the bow down to begin the process over. Under this arrangement the boat will be heeled but balanced, and you will slowly wallow sideways. Heaving-to is no fun, but it will keep you upright and safe. Practice the procedure several times in light breezes so you will know what to do should it become necessary.

- Lying ahull: It's another hunker-down tactic that puts the boat at an angle to wind and sea, but without any sails set. Instead, a sea anchor is set on a bridle either at the bow or abeam, so the boat will stream to it. There are no hard and fast rules about where it needs to be set, since all boats act differently under changing conditions, so you need to practice to determine what angle is best for your vessel.

- Steering at an angle: Increasing wind causes the sea to build which makes it more difficult for boats with a short waterline like small trailerable cruisers to make headway. Large swells and waves not only will shake up the crew, but they will considerably impede or reverse forward progress. Do not approach a large wave head-on, because you will not have the momentum to continue, and once in the trough, the next wave may push you sideways and knock you down. The trick is to stop sailing the closest possible angle to the wind, but to crack off a few degrees, which will do two things: It increases the speed and your boat's ability to "punch through" the chop while it simultaneously creates a shallower angle to the crests, so the boat can actually climb the waves. When going down the back of a wave, fall off a little and when approaching the next wave, point the boat slightly upwind, which creates a wake that resembles an S-line. Get into the rhythm and you will be able to make good some distance to weather even if in very bad conditions.

There are countless stories about people who circumnavigated without so much as a whiff of a storm. But equally, there are countless tales of people getting clobbered right outside their own harbor because they neglected to prepare for heavy weather. These you find in the Coast Guard reports and many of them have a bad ending. Be prudent, prepare, practice and talk the crew through the steps of each maneuver before it gets dicey. Once the breeze is up, it is near impossible to communicate clearly by voice, because it gets too loud on board and a boat bucking a raging sea won't help. But if everyone knows what to do, how and when, the confidence level of all involved parties is much higher and with it the safety of boat and crew.

## ➤ CREW OVERBOARD ≺

Perhaps Tony Gibbs said it best in his book *The Coastal Cruiser*: "There is almost never an adequate excuse for someone's falling overboard. It is nearly always carelessness, sometimes equipment failure, but it should not have happened." Although Gibbs is absolutely right, people do fall overboard and not all of them live to tell the tale. It's one of the most dreaded and lethal emergencies that can befall boaters. In 2004, the U.S. Coast Guard's recreational boating accident statistics tracked 488 fall-overboard incidents that resulted in 199 deaths, a 40-percent fatality rate. Numbers don't lie but they should not scare, either. They serve as a reminder that practice and preparedness will go a long way towards safe and enjoyable boating.

If someone falls overboard, the first rule is: Don't panic. You need your nerves and your skills to execute a basic maneuver that breaks down into several steps with the lone goal to get the victim on board as quickly as possible. The beautiful thing is that there is no single right or wrong way, as the repeated tests of various maneuvers and pieces of gear proved during the Crew Overboard Symposium of 2005 that was organized by some of the world's most knowledgeable experts. How you go about returning, stopping and retrieving the victim depends on the type of boat you sail, the conditions you encounter, your crew and your comfort zone.

Without going into all the details, the Crew Overboard maneuvers can be divided into turning and point-of-sail methods. While the former—called the *Quick Stop* and the *Fast Return*—keep the boat in closer proximity to the victim, they require a high degree of boat handling skill and are therefore more difficult to execute properly for an untrained crew. Point-of-sail maneuvers like the *Figure Eight* and the *Deep Beam Reach* are easier to perform, hence they are being taught in sailing classes. However, because they don't stop the boat right away, they put more distance between the victim and the rescuers.

Once you are stopped near the victim, the real fun starts, which is getting the person back on board. Throwing a Type IV flotation device, a throw rope, or a Lifesling that's connected to the boat establishes contact, but what if the victim is injured, hypothermic, overweight or otherwise incapacitated and can't climb back on board by him/herself?

The least you can do is deploy a swim ladder or an elevator line or in case of serious injury, rig a block-and tackle system on a spare halyard and a primary winch to hoist the victim back on board. Crew overboard rescues don't follow scripts, so keeping an open mind and mastering different techniques is more important than buying every gadget on the market or watching videos. "Boathandling skills," as one expert succinctly put it, "will trump doctrine every time." Mandatory refresher courses for crew-overboard recoveries are not likely to happen, so you are on your own, but the following advice should help you develop your own best practice for the execution of a crew overboard maneuver:

- Know your boat. Skipper and crew should be familiar with their craft in different conditions and know how long it takes to come to a stop in flat and choppy water.
- Experiment. Try down-speed maneuvers and become familiar with the turning ability of your vessel. If it has a keel it'll carry momentum longer and farther than a boat with a combination of water ballast and centerboard.
- Keep it simple. Many skippers like the deep beam reach return, because it only involves two points of sail and gives you options to bear off or head up to control speed and position relative to the person in the water.
- Keep a lookout. Spotting the victim and turning back is extremely important when you are on a fast point of sail like a beam reach.
- Lose the jib. If possible, douse or furl the jib before picking up the victim. It frees crew for spotting and recovering the victim and prevents foul-ups or injuries resulting from flogging sheets. If your boat won't sail to weather under main alone, choose your point of sail accordingly.
- Practice. Put a live person in the water. Man-overboard drills with cushions and boathooks are not enough. You'll be surprised how much more difficult it is to get a 200-pound adult in water-logged gear on board—maybe even over the lifelines—than a two-pound piece of Styrofoam.
- Keep an open mind. Learn and practice different techniques. Not all methods suit all types of boats and points of sail equally well.
- Fire up the engine if necessary. Maneuvers can get sloppy if people are stressed out and the assistance of an engine can substantially speed up the return, especially if the boat is downwind of the victim.
- Be selective. You won't have enough storage for a truck-load of gear. Assess what works for you, learn how it works, teach your crew, and store it so you can get to it quickly in an emergency.

- Establish a chain of command. Even on expertly crewed boats a lack of leadership produces chaos. Think about the unthinkable, too: Who's going to get the skipper out of the drink?
- Prepare. Take some time to go over the procedures while still at the dock. A briefed crew will work more efficiently.
- Improvise. Modifying equipment, e.g. extending a halyard or re-reefing it to reach a stronger winch can save lives. Make sure you have supplies (blocks, line, shackles) at hand.
- Put the victim in the lee. You can't throw a line to weather with any accuracy when it blows, and a boat drifts much faster than anyone can swim with boots, foulies and an inflated PFD.
- Be smart. If your boat has a swim step or scoop on the stern, use it to retrieve the victim.
- Mind the motion. Even with all sails down, a hull's windage pushes the boat along, which can make recovery difficult in rough conditions.
- Elevator lines, rigged between a clamp and a winch, can work in absence of a boarding ladder, but the victim needs additional support by grabbing toerail, lifelines, shrouds or a heavy line from the cockpit.
- Consider a nighttime nightmare. Can you spot a person in the water in the dark? Personal safety lights or strobe lights that are either attached to the PFD or thrown overboard as a buoy can make a difference. Alternatively, a clip-on chemstick can be used.
- Last but not least: Wear your PFD and have your crew do the same. It's the single most important lifesaver for someone who's fallen in the drink.

## ➤ LIGHT-AIR SKILLS ◄

If a crew in the water or heavy-weather sailing represents the high-adrenaline aspect of sailing, keeping the boat moving along in light air requires subtle skills, such as economical and nimble movements by the crew, good observation of the surroundings by the skipper and a great deal of concentration by all who handle sail trim. While in most parts of the country days of bone-rattling storms and utter calms are rare, you'd be surprised how many days there are with light air, so there is merit in developing the necessary skills.

In a zephyr skippers of larger and heavier boats won't even bother to take the sail covers off. If they go, they go under steam. But this is where the lighter displacement of a trailerable sailboat can make a big difference, because it will respond to the slightest puffs and it can be tacked quickly on the slightest wind shifts. This assumes that you haven't loaded it down with tons of stuff and turned it into a heavy-displacement vessel with a short waterline. Here are a few pointers for turning the slightest puff into propulsion for your boat:

- Minimize the crew's motion on the boat by asking everyone to move as little as possible. In an anemic breeze, uncoordinated rocking of the boat spills the wind from the sails, which will stop you dead in your tracks.
- Ask the crew to position themselves forward in the cockpit to help get the stern out of the water and minimize drag.
- Continuously check your masthead fly and the woolen telltales in your jib and at the leech of the mainsail to determine the direction of the breeze and the airflow across your sails. Light air is shifty and makes it necessary to constantly adjust course and sail trim.
- Loosen the sail control lines (down- and outhaul, boom vang and mainsheet). You can even ease the jib and the main halyards an inch or two to give the sails more camber.
- Move crew weight to the leeward side to create heel and reduce the drag by minimizing the wetted surface.
- Don't over-trim your sails. Light air requires a light touch.
- Once you have headway, steer gently. Unnecessary jerks on the tiller will turn the rudder harshly, which compromises the flow around the rudder blade and slows down the boat.
- If your boat lives in the water, make sure your bottom is

clean. There's nothing like a colony of budding barnacles to impede progress.

- If even the last bit of breeze disappears before you are home, drop your sails and crank the outboard. You'll still use less fossil fuel than the guy who has to move a 20-ton cruising vessel.

Now let's pause for a moment and check what we've learned thus far. We should be able to get away from our slip without banging into other boats, docks, or nearby piers; we should also manage to return and tie up without crashing the boat. We know what it takes to do a reasonably good repair job on the boat if we hit something and begin to take on water. We know how to reef the sails and how to apply some storm tactics if the going gets really rough, and we know what to practice to perfect a crew overboard maneuver in case we need to perform one. And we have discussed the do's and don'ts of light-air sailing to get the most out of our sailboat. We are almost ready to select and buy the right safety equipment. But before we do that, let us talk about two other mishaps that might occur on trailerable sailboats, at least every now and then, so you will have some idea about preventing or minimizing damage if either one happens to you.

## ➤ BROKEN STANDING RIGGING ◄

Besides sinking, one of the most spectacular mishaps on a sailboat is a dismasting. Millions of TV viewers got a taste of it watching the America's Cup finals in 2003. Down 0-3, the overmatched New Zealand defenders tried to make something happen against the Swiss challengers when their mast snapped on the third upwind leg of the race. Not only did it stop them dead but it left them with a tangled mess of broken carbon fiber and wires to sort out, while their opponent coasted to an easy win. And it wasn't even blowing hard.

A trailerable sailboat is not a finely tuned America's Cup

yacht, but if the wrong part breaks at the wrong time, you too could be forced to deal with a stick that's less than upright. But for the average cruiser the likelihood of dismasting can be greatly reduced with simple regular maintenance checks, and by taking proper care of the stays and shrouds when raising the mast. It's a dirty little trailerboating secret, but most dismastings go back to careless handling of spars and rigging in the parking lot. A nicked shroud, a bent bolt, a forgotten O-ring or cotter pin are trivial, but very real sources of immense trouble later on.

If you do routine inspections of your stays and shrouds, examining them for broken wire strands, burrs, corrosion etc., you can nip the possibility of breakage in the bud. In addition, be very careful not to kink the stays or shrouds when raising the mast. Kinks can weaken the wire strands that make up the standing rigging, thereby increasing the possibility that it will break.

To illustrate the point that some dismastings don't occur because of broken stays and shrouds, but as a result of sheer stupidity, I offer this example: luck was with us as my nephew and I sailed along with three other boats from Perdido Bay, Alabama, down the Intracoastal Waterway to Redfish Point near Pensacola, Florida. It was a fantastic sail on a starboard reach with 10- to 12-knot breezes all the way. We arrived at Redfish Point just about dinnertime. We dropped our sails and all the crews rafted up to recap the day and eat. While rafted up, I accidentally raised the turnbuckle boots that covered the shroud turnbuckles on the port side of the boat. That's when I noticed that I had forgotten to insert the cotter pins that hold the turnbuckles in place. My heart sank to my stomach. If I had tacked at any time during the day, the rig force would have shifted from the starboard shrouds to the port side shrouds, and my mast could have come crashing down. Apparently, in my haste to raise the mast and put the boat in the water, I had neglected to check everything properly. Only a steady breeze over the starboard bow that allowed us to sail on port tack all the time had saved my mast. Don't repeat my mistake and make sure to check the rigging carefully before leaving. Five minutes spent on inspecting and taping off cotter pins or O-rings with duct tape can save you days of agonizing repairs (not to mention hundreds of dollars) and a lifetime of embarrassment.

- A broken headstay: Let's say it is a wonderful, sunny day with a steady breeze of 18 knots. You are sailing on a broad reach. As you approach the sailing club, you come about to head back to your slip. You uncleat the jib sheet, push the tiller to leeward, and turn the boat through the wind. As the boat comes about, the main fills and you trim the jib sheet and cleat it. Just as the sails fill, you hear a treacherous "ping," and the headstay goes slack and falls to the deck. Not good. But if you act quickly you might be able to prevent the stick from coming down, too. The trick is to immediately take the strain off the compromised wire because only a strained stay or shroud will brake. And here's why you stand more than a fighting chance: The jib's luff will most likely hold the mast upright for a few moments. Fall off immediately (hopefully you have enough room to do so) and ease the main sheet, so the wind keeps forward pressure on the mast, grab a free halyard (genoa, spinnaker or the spinnaker pole's topping lift) and run it to the stemhead fitting. Keep the jib up, drop the main and start the engine to make a beeline back to safety.
- A broken backstay: This case could be far less dramatic than a broken forestay unless, of course, you are heading downwind with full canvas flying. In this case, reverse the procedure by heading up and turning the boat's bow into the wind. Drop the jib and sheet in the main to hold the mast upright while you think about possible repairs. If there is no easy way to fix the problem, strike all sails and get under way under motor. If that isn't an option, drop the main and use the main halyard to jury rig a backstay, so you can proceed under jib.
- A broken shroud: If a shroud snaps, you need a bit of good luck to escape the worst-case scenario, because most likely it

will be the windward shroud that goes in a moment when you can ill afford it. Quick-witted action might be the only measure that can help prevent the stick from going over the leeward side. If you can, crash-tack the boat to put the broken shroud on the leeward side and ease all sheets immediately. If you accomplished that and the mast still stands, you are okay. If your boat has a mast that's stepped on the keel the deck might be strong enough to hold it upright for a few moments, a hope that's impossible to maintain if the stick is stepped on deck, which is very common on small trailerboats to open up the space down below. Drop your sails and motor back perhaps with a jury-rigged shroud from a spare halyard.

• What if the mast breaks high above deck? The broken piece will come down and hit the water next to the hull. Get the mess back on board if you can, and try to save the sails from tearing. If that is not possible and the broken piece of the mast extrusion is bouncing wildly in rough seas, trying to punch a hole into the hull, you need to cut the wires that still hold it and scuttle it before it does more damage. A good set of wire cutters should be at hand for this specific purpose. If you manage to salvage the sails and you have enough of a stump left, it might be possible to jury rig some sail plan by lashing the whisker or spinnaker pole to extend the mast. If successful, a jury rig would allow you to continue under your own power and without an engine, sailing on a deep beam reach or downwind to reach the next harbor. Countless cruisers who were dismasted in the middle of the ocean managed to sail thousands of miles to safety under jury rig.

Remember to take care of your stays and shrouds and inspect them often. Do it every spring before commissioning the boat, as part of your routine maintenance. Crevice corrosion usually builds inside the lower swage fittings where water accumulates. The cheap trick, of course, is to reverse the shrouds and stays, turning them upside down like budget racers do with their old halyards prior to the racing season in the hope to get some more useful life out of them. And be watchful when stepping and unstepping the mast, so you don't compromise the standing rigging. The golden rule is to replace the wires "when necessary." A set of stays and shrouds for a trailerable sailboat are a small expense compared to a new mast, so replacing standing rigging often is better.

## ➤ A BROKEN RUDDER ≺

Properly maintained and designed rudders rarely break by themselves. A broken rudder usually is a consequence of bad luck, bad craftsmanship or shoddy sailing, like hitting an unseen submerged object or running hard aground. Regardless of the cause, a broken rudder means you lose steerage and you need to stop sailing at once. If the foil snaps off, you will know immediately because you'll lose all response from the helm and the boat will most likely round up. First order of business should be dousing your sails immediately to assess the damage and regain control. The easiest and most logical thing to do is start your engine. If it's an outboard, you're in good shape because you will have a way to steer the vessel home, or at least back to shore for repairs. If you don't have a motor, or if it's an inboard engine that requires a functioning rudder, or if you can't get it started, you will have to use some ingenuity to rig a temporary rudder by using a paddle or some other piece of equipment you have on board. The legendary yarns talk about McGyver types, who can build an emergency rudder from the lid of a cooler or a cabin door and a dinghy oar that's lashed to the sternrail where it dutifully serves for the next 1,500 miles. Once the temporary rudder is in place and you are ready to proceed, be cautious about the amount of canvas you hoist, because a jury-rigged rudder probably won't stand up to a lot of pressure.

If possible, equip your sailboat with a kick-up rudder. It will greatly reduce the probability of rudder damage in case of contact with submerged objects or other obstacles by simply riding up and over most submerged objects you might encounter. If your trailerable sailboat does not come standard with a kick-up rudder, but it is offered as an option, consider that option. You will be glad you did.

Now that we have discussed some of the more typical emergency situations you might encounter on your trailerable sailboat, don't panic. The described situations don't happen every time you take your sailboat out. There are legions of sailors who have been happily sailing their boats for years, even decades without ever having to deal with any of that stuff. Bad things most likely won't happen to the prepared sailor. And if they do, the consequences will be much less dramatic.

## ➤ SUMMARY ◄

Probably the most frequent cause of all accidents is complacency. After 25 years of sailing, I have learned that foul weather seeks human complacency as its companion. Sailboats require us to be alert at all times, even at anchor. I can imagine nothing more satisfying than being completely relaxed, with all senses on high alert. It is in just such a state that one is wide awake and fully receptive to all stimuli. I actually pity the sailor who isn't confidently alert, and who isn't prepared to deal with whatever the elements cook up. He will not enjoy sailing for long, but tire of the level of attention that is required. He will be happier playing golf, mowing the lawn or simply turning an ignition key and driving a powerboat.

The best advice I can provide is to get to know your own limits, and those of your boat. Don't undertake a voyage, however short it might be, that could take you beyond your ability, or the limits of your boat. If you are going on a cruise, think about the risks that may be involved before you leave shore. Although you will not be able to anticipate every situation, try to prepare as much as possible. Think, plan, and practice and solving problems will become second nature, even and especially before they become critical.

# 6

# *The Necessities*

*Ships, I may say, when not at sea, are always being fitted out or refitted or worked over in some way; they are never complete; work on them is never done, they are ceaselessly, relentlessly demanding, and if you waited until every job was finished you would not put to sea at all.*

ANN DAVISON, My Ship is So Small

## ➤ INTRODUCTION ≺

Before you hoist your sails, it's your captain's duty to remember that everyone on board assumes that you have taken all reasonable steps to make the voyage a safe one. Not only do family and friends on your sailboat expect this, so do the people on other boats around you, and the authorities. And the authorities are requiring boaters to bring a fair number of safety items, from personal flotation to communication and other equipment.

An experienced boater knows that legal requirements are nothing more than basic guidelines, a minimum defined by the letter of the law that will keep you out of trouble, at least when the Coast Guard comes knocking to do an on-board inspection. But beyond that, you are likely to add other safety items that make your vessel safe for your style of sailing and complement your skills and the sailing venues you frequent. But don't assume that indulgence in gadgetry will automatically solve all your problems. Safe boating begins with solid skills, keeping a lookout and respecting the weather.

When shopping for gear, spend some time to think about how you will deploy it, where you will stow it and how you can educate your crew to become adept in its use as well. And always keep the weight factor in mind. Lots of gear is cool and useful, but how will it affect your boat's performance?

## ➤ PERSONAL FLOTATION DEVICES ◄

Call them what you will: life jackets, life vests or Personal Flotation Devices (PFDs). They all do the same—keeping people afloat—and they are required by U.S. Coast Guard regulations. Somehow (and to nobody's surprise) they have emerged as the single-most effective means to save the lives of victims who end up in the water against their own volition. A whopping 80 percent of U.S. recreational boating drowning fatalities could probably have been prevented if the victims would have worn PFDs.

On recreational vessels there must be at least one Coast Guard approved personal flotation device of Type I, II, III or V for each person on the boat. In addition, boats of 16 feet or longer must have at least one Type IV, throwable PFD aboard. That's all a bit ambiguous, but the regulations also say that the device must be approved by the Coast Guard, in good and serviceable condition and must fit the person who wears it. Regulations by state might differ slightly, but as a general rule, assume that kids under the age of 13 should wear a suitable PFD when on deck while under way. Important for children's PFDs is their weight rating, which is noted on the label of the product. The Coast Guard rates PFDs by Type (I, II, III, IV and V) but that doesn't necessarily tell you what to buy.

The vest must be right for the person and the sailing style, which in our case requires good fit and relative freedom of movement. Great choices are automatically or manually inflatable vests, which are also available as belt packs. These must be worn at all times, but they give the wearer the freedom to move without adding bulk. However, they are pricey, so check out alternatives, like water sport vests made of foam with a nice snug fit.

Generally, these are Type III vests. They are considerably more affordable than inflatables, but are not designed to turn an unconscious victim on his/her back when afloat. Also, they add bulk and cause sweating in hot weather or during physical activities on board.

For occasional company you always can buy a few bulky, cheap Type II vests with huge collars that live in the lazarette until needed. While they'll keep the wearer afloat, they certainly won't win a fashion price or a commendation for comfort.

Manufacturers have begun to offer hybrid products that double as jackets and life vests called swim shirts (for kids) or float coats and flotation jackets (for adults). Comfortable, practical and effective they might be, but they only are accepted by the Coast Guard as a proper PFD if worn.

For throwable Type IV PFDs there's one strong contender among all the available products such as float cushions, ring or horseshoe buoys, called the Lifesling. Technically it's a Type V device with a Type-IV performance and it is mounted on the stern-rail for quick access. Different models are available, including one that automatically inflates upon contact with water, but every one stays connected to the boat with a long line and can be rigged to hoist the victim back aboard.

If you are doing night sailing, your PFDs should have small water-activated flashlights and whistles attached on them so that a crew that ends up in the drink can be spotted in poor visibility or darkness.

I could give you a long lecture about the obvious benefits of wearing personal flotation devices on the boat. But I also know that there are some who always find excuses for not wearing a PFD, so at least let me strongly urge you to keep your PFDs neatly stored in a readily accessible place. In other words, don't stuff them down in a storage area with lots of other things on top of them.

## ➤ VHF RADIO ≺

In some solo sailors' minds the mere fact of having a radio on board is an implicit acknowledgement of the intention to screw up and having to call for help. If you venture out on a boat by yourself, they argue, you have to be able to extricate yourself from the trouble that might befall you. If you're not sure, simply don't go. It is a tough stance that existed long before the discussions about making foolish weekend adventurers pay for their rescues, if it can be proven that they got into harm's way despite prior warnings about dangerous conditions and calculated that a call on Channel 16 (or to 911 via cell phone) will save them.

Categorically rejecting outside communications and simply relying on it to get out of trouble are extreme positions on either side of the spectrum and between them is where you will find the majority of boaters. Always remember that as the owner/skipper of a boat you are personally responsible for the safety of the boat and the people who are sailing with you. *Don't rely on mobile phones.* Even on a relatively small body of water like San Francisco Bay, there are many dead spots without adequate service. If you sail in coastal waters or offshore, forget a cell phone as a reliable emergency communication device.

With today's VHF radios that are readily available for less than $200, there is no reason not to have one, at least a compact portable. The very least one can say about VHF radios is that they are convenient and practical. Some common uses are:

- Calling for help in an emergency
- Checking weather reports
- Communicating with fellow boaters and commercial shipping
- Checking in with the race committee whether you participate in a regatta or just want to make sure you stay clear of others who do
- Hailing drawbridge operators to request passage

- Talking to the marina office if you are coming in from the water and need a berth
- Asking the harbor launch to come out to your mooring to shuttle you and your passengers to the dock.

The choice of radios is staggering, both in terms of features and price. Technology has advanced in leaps and bounds and like all electronics VHF radios are subject to shrinking in size while bulging with features that are nearly the same on portables and fixed-mount models, except that portables have much less transmit power (max. 6 watts vs. 25 watts on fixed models) and are limited by their battery life.

Depending on conditions, the range of a portable VHF with an integrated antenna does not exceed 5 miles line of sight by very much, while a fixed VHF with 25 watts of transmitting power and an antenna up on the masthead can reach 15-20 miles. Because antenna height correlates to range, portables that are connected to an external mast-mounted antenna will get better transmission range.

Technology constantly improves radio performance. Here are some details to look for in a VHF radio:

- Multi-band capabilities: Some radios have Family Radio Service (FRS) Aircraft Band or AM/FM integrated, which adds to their versatility. This is important since VHF radios by law are only intended for ship-to-ship or ship-to-shore communication.
- Weather Alerts: Automatic detection of NOAA's weather warnings keeps you abreast of the latest weather developments. Specific Area Message Encoding (S.A.M.E.) limits the forecasts you receive to the geographic area you are in.
- Battery Life: All modern portable VHFs come with a rechargeable battery. Lithium-Ion batteries last the longest, but Nickel Metal Hydride in cheaper models is OK, too. A tray for alkaline batteries comes in handy as a backup

when you run out of juice and don't have the time or the ability to recharge the radio.

- Waterproofness: Waterproof sounds good as a sales argument for portable VHFs and is supported by arcane ratings codes (JIS-4, IPX-7 etc.) but it's relative. Most people never use a radio under water and dropping it overboard, as it might happen, ends the product's useful life in virtually all cases. As a rule, the more expensive the radio, the "more waterproof" it is, meaning that it withstands deeper immersion for a longer period. But usually, a radio that's resistant to splash water will do. If it gets any wetter than that, keeping it in a waterproof bag might be the way to go.

- Digital Selective Calling: Fixed VHF now have DSC capabilities, which means they can be hooked up to a GPS to transmit the boat's position along with the vessel's identity and (optional) encrypted information about the type of emergency. This service requires registration of the radio to obtain a so-called Maritime Mobile Service Identity number (MMSI).

- Scanning functions: Several useful scanning modes (e.g. programmable, priority, dual, and tri-watch) make it easy to scan and listen to important channels, including Channel 16, Channel 9, plus whatever channel(s) the skipper decides to select.

- External speaker: The cockpit of a small boat in windy conditions is a noisy place so an external speaker that's connected to a VHF radio that is mounted below deck makes sense to listen to radio traffic while sailing the boat.

- External antenna: A fixed VHF will need an external antenna, and a portable model will benefit from it, because it improves the range by mounting it high up in the mast. Select a short whip antenna (stainless steel) with at least 3 dB of gain, which doubles the signal's strength. However, the drawback is that the coaxial cable that connects the antenna and radio will reduce some of that gain. The solution is to use larger coax cable for long runs.

In summary, you should have a VHF radio on your trailerable sail-boat. Ideally, you have a fixed VHF radio down below and a portable as a backup in the cockpit. It is, at the very least, a prac-tical communication device and in extreme cases it might save lives or prevent material loss either for you or other boaters. With-out a VHF radio you are not only sailing small, you also might be sailing dangerously.

## ➤ FIRST-AID KITS ≺

Nobody wants to think about injuries when casting off from the dock to take advantage of a pleasant day on the water for two rea-sons: One, the goal is to enjoy the time out on the water, and two, sailing is not known to be a dangerous sport. Still, small medical emergencies can and do happen, but with proper attention they stay small. One of the most common reasons to have some med-ical kit on board is keeping a stash of Aspirin and Dramamine handy to combat headaches and motion sickness.

Unless you are planning to cross an ocean and be away from any professional help for days or weeks, selecting a medical kit for a trailerable sailboat is not a highly scientific process. The fol-lowing guidelines can help you organize your priorities and find what you need for your personal style of boating and to treat peo-ple for routine sickness or injury. In the event of something more serious, most medical kits only provide the means for emergency treatment before professional care is available.

- Organization: A kit must be designed so you find what you need to treat the problem with the proper means, e.g. the right size band-aid for a cut, the proper cream for a burn etc. Therefore good kits are compartmentalized not by items, but by injury type that needs to be treated and have labeled, waterproof, transparent and re-sealable storage bags inside. Know what you need and find it quickly.

- Product choice: Select a medical kit that was designed for use under marine conditions.
- Instructions: Unless you are a medical professional, bring a good manual or first-aid booklet that succinctly explains in layman terms what you need to know to treat basic emergencies.
- Contents: What kind of injuries can occur on a sailboat? This is a bit of a worst-case scenario and doesn't mean that it will happen, but be prepared to deal with burns, cuts, lacerations, shock, abrasions, sprains and in rare cases fractures. Good kits are prepackaged for those types of emergencies with neatly labeled packs.
- Size: To choose the right size of the kit, consider how many people are sailing on your boat and for how long. On a trailerable sailboat in our category, small kits that contain supplies for two to four people for up to six days should be plenty.
- Storage: Medical supplies should be kept dry and clean. They need to be packaged in a protective bag, preferably a sturdy case with a zipper and handles that floats. Don't settle for cheap plastic boxes like you see in car kits.
- Motion sickness: preventing motion sickness is one thing, treating it is another. And those who talk from experience will recommend prophylactic approach any day. Eat light and don't drink alcohol before going on a trip that might include some rough sailing. If *mal de mer* still is a threat, there's a large number of products available to treat it, but not all are effective for everyone. Some swear by drugs like Bonine or Granny's Ginger Caps that need to be taken before the symptoms show up. Others like elastic or electrical acupressure bands that are worn around the wrists and don't require pre-medication.

## ➤ FIRE EXTINGUISHERS ◄

The best way to prevent a fire on a sailboat is to keep things clean and orderly. This means that in addition to making sure that oil, gasoline, and other flammable liquids are properly stored, you should make every effort to keep the bilge clean and free of conditions that might contribute to a fire. If you are at all like me, you will be quite fastidious about keeping your sailboat shipshape.

A trailerable sailboat has fewer built-in potential fire hazards than a much larger one that is loaded down with fuel and electrical systems. In addition, fire extinguishers on a trailerable sailboat will certainly be closer to the source of trouble than on a larger boat. Sometimes, however, fires do happen, and you should be prepared to deal with them quickly and effectively.

Fires are classified as Class "A," Class "B," or Class "C," based on the type of material involved. Class "A" fires involve ordinary combustible materials such as wood, paper and cloth. These fires can effectively be extinguished by water, so have a bucket with a line attached to it handy for throwing over the side and scooping up water. Class "B" fires result from the ignition of petroleum products, grease, and similar substances, while Class "C" fires are electrical fires.

This classification also applies to fire extinguishers. If the rating was issued by Underwriter Laboratories, it includes a number that indicates the extinguishing capacity. This is a bit confusing, since the Coast Guard uses a different terminology, B-I and B-II. Coast Guard Regulations require one B-I fire extinguisher on boats of up to 26 feet in length that have an enclosed engine compartment, living spaces or permanent fuel tanks.

Then there is the question of what kind of agent the fire extinguisher should contain. Nontoxic, dry chemical is the most widely used on trailerable sailboats. These fire extinguishers are portable and quite inexpensive, two facts which account for their popularity. These extinguishers are appropriate for Class B and

Class C fires. You should be aware that when discharged, they leave a powdery residue, which can be difficult to clean up. Dry chemical agents can include sodium bicarbonate or mono-ammonium phosphate. Think about what kind of fire you could most likely encounter on your boat and choose the extinguisher's agent accordingly. Carbon Dioxide is good for fires of class B and C; FE-241 and FM-200 replace Halon and leave no residue, but are more expensive and allegedly also less effective; Halotron is safe for electrical fires and won't damage electronics with residue; Tri-Class Dry Chemical, as the name suggests, can be used to extinguish all three classes of fires, but is corrosive and hard to clean up. Another point to consider is the shelf life of the extinguisher. Will you shell out the money for a rechargeable model or do you stick with the throw-away concept and buy a cheap disposable model?

A word about activation and mounting brackets: Fire extinguishers need to be accessible in a case of emergency. Time is of the essence for fighting even the smallest of fires, so there can't be any delays in activating the extinguisher. The crew should be familiar with its operation, which is likely to require the removal of a pin and pulling a trigger. Mounting brackets should be sturdy and made of non-corrosive metal rather than plastic. Make sure they hold the extinguisher so it can be mounted in the right spot, which on a small trailerable boat most likely also is a tight spot.

On a trailerable sailboat, especially one that has an outboard engine, you are fine with two fire extinguishers: one mounted in the cabin and one in the cockpit under a cockpit seat that also can be used to deal with a fire in the galley if you can't get to the one in the cabin.

Fires don't care where you are sailing, and it is just as difficult for a fire truck to get to the middle of the lake or to go offshore. Again, my best advice is to keep your sailboat clean and orderly. By doing so you most likely won't have to deal with a fire onboard.

## ➤ TOOLS ≺

Pick almost any weekend and visit the nearest facility where trailerable sailboats are berthed or stored on their trailers. What you will immediately notice is that the skippers of boats that are not sailing are busy with jobs like caulking, screwing, tightening, loosening, hammering, sawing, sewing, mopping, washing, inspecting, and polishing. It seems that when we are not sailing our boats, we are invariably tinkering with them.

Pay special attention to the various implements fellow boaters are using: screwdrivers, hammers, needle-nose pliers, slip-joint pliers, vice grips, socket wrenches, sanding blocks, drills, caulking guns, hacksaws, and wire cutters, to mention only a few. These people will be sewing sails and sail covers, inserting cotter pins, adjusting stays and shrouds, drilling holes, inspecting running rigging, rebuilding fresh-water pumps, and checking electrical systems.

You won't be able to escape the fact that you will need a basic tool kit on your boat; there is always something that needs to be done and even if there isn't, you still will want to fiddle with something. It's a sailor's compulsion, plain and simple. And that doesn't even begin to account for the things that can break while under way. Like a medical kit for the crew, a well-sorted tool box is an essential piece of gear for the boat, and the boat's safety. You will notice that tools seem to breed and multiply. Often a new project means buying a new tool, which then joins the others in the lazarette. You will see.

**Contents of a Basic Sailboat Tool Kit**

**Tools**

Pliers; slip-joint, needle-nose, and vice grip
Standard, slot-head screwdriver
Phillips-head screwdriver
Crescent wrench
Hammer
Hacksaw
Wire cutters

Hand or cordless drill and assorted bits    *bucket*
Files; wood and metal
Tape measure
Socket wrenches
Spark plug socket set
Assorted nuts, screws, and bolts
Roll of good, strong wire
Needle and thread for sail repair

**Spare Parts and Supplies**
Spark plug
Shear and cotter pins
Rip-stop tape
Corks
Hose clamps
Electrical tape
Sailkote lubricant
Silicone sealant

## ➤ DISTRESS SIGNALS ◄

For operation in coastal waters, all sailboats over 16 feet in length are required to carry USCG-approved visual distress signals that must have a manufacturing date no older than 42 months, so look for the printed date on the outside of the flare. Boats under 16 feet must have night distress signals when operating after dark. Even if you may never sail the U.S. coast, state and local regulations may require visual distress signals on your sailboat. When not absolutely required by any agency, they are, nevertheless, something you should have on board.

### Visual Signals

There is a range of visual distress signals available—from flags to electric SOS lights—but the most important ones are pyrotechnic signals, handheld or fired in the air with a dedicated flare gun.

Boats in our size range are required to carry a three-day/night supply of pyrotechnic devices with the option to substitute an orange
distress flag for day use and a white signal light at night. Two tips
from seasoned offshore sailors should be mentioned here: If you
are concerned about your safety and your ability to alert fellow
boaters and rescue units, invest in SOLAS (Safety of Life at Sea)
compliant flares. They cost more but they are designed for tough
offshore conditions, meaning they are waterproof, easy to set off
and more visible from afar because of their brightness. If your
boating style is more casual, you still should have flares aboard,
but you might find that pre-packaged kits that contain flares and a
launcher are sufficient. These kits come in a variety of sizes and
require an investment of $50-$100. The second tip is to hang on to
old and outdated flares (especially if they are SOLAS compliant)
because they don't go bad quickly. In fact, having good and use-
able old flares in the stockpile on board in addition to legally correct ones might make a difference because most likely they'll
work, thus giving you more firepower to attract attention.

At any rate, flares must be handy when they are needed, yet
they also should live in a protected, dry spot, which means they
are a typical lazarette item. In some states a flare gun may be considered to be a firearm and, therefore, subject to licensing. Check
local regulations to learn the requirements for your area.

Other items you could consider as visual distress signals are
orange distress flags with a black square and a black dot printed
on them and super-bright lights flashing the SOS Morse code.
Small but useful are the two attributes that apply to a pocket mirror that allows distressed mariners to re-direct sunlight toward
aircraft or other boaters to attract attention.

### Acoustic Signals

According to USCG regulations, sailboats of more than 40 feet in
length must carry a bell, whistle, or some other device to signal
their position in poor visibility or announce their intentions

(course changes etc.) acoustically. Up to 40 feet the law does not require a sound device, but it's still a good idea to have one on board. Ozone-safe air horns, whistles, electric handheld horns, even an old-fashioned bell are all compact, cheap and easy to use, so if someone can't see you at least they might hear you and start paying attention.

Besides, it's "sound practice" to give one blast with a horn when leaving the marina and entering the main channel from behind a row of docks or a breakwater. Let's hope you never end up like a Gloucester fishing smack anchored out at the Grand Banks in fog thick as pea soup having to sound your horn or bell continuously to alert surrounding boats or approaching cargo ships of your presence . . .

## ➢ PADDLES ≺

Don't feel embarrassed for having a paddle on your boat. Just be thankful that a paddle can move you along if the wind disappears and your outboard motor won't start or you have to move the stern a few feet to reach that docking line that dangles from a pylon at your dock. Moving a 2000-pound boat over any distance by paddle won't be easy, but at least you have a chance to do something if everything else fails. Besides, remember that a paddle can be jury-rigged as an emergency rudder, so there's your most compelling reason why you should keep one board.

## ➢ ANCHOR(S) AND LINE ≺

Even if you'd never consider spending a night at anchor or dropping the hook in a nice spot to go for a swim or have some civilized lunch, don't leave the dock without a reliable anchor and some sturdy rode.

## Anchors

What type of anchor (Danforth, CQR, claw or plow-type) is best for you depends on the sailing venue and the anchoring grounds found there. Danforth anchors are always popular and there are very good products on the market that provide great holding power, can be disassembled for storage and are relatively light (less than 10 pounds for boats up to 25 feet). But they won't work so well on rocky, muddy and grassy bottoms, so your best bet might be a combination of two anchors, e.g. one Danforth and a CQR that complement each other. Consult the experts at your marine supply store to find what's right for you.

## Rode

Any anchor is only as good as its weakest link and that's the line and chain that connects it to the boat. Of course, 200 feet of high-test chain would be safest, but for a small boat that is too much weight to be carrying in the bow. Plus, most likely, your boat won't have an electric windlass so bringing it all back on board is a lot of back-breaking work, especially when you anchor in 30 feet of water.

On the other hand, ditching the chain for the same length of three-stranded nylon rope is tempting, because the advantages are clear: It's cheap, it's light, it stretches to absorb shock loads, and it's easy to stow. But line can and will chafe on rocky bottom and provides no weight that helps the anchor to dig into the ground and keep the boat's pull near horizontal.

The sensible compromise is a combined nylon line/galvanized high-test chain rode with a professionally spliced link between both that does away with the thimble and the galvanized shackle.

To size the rode, consider ⅛ of an inch of nylon line for every 9 feet of boat length and half that for proof coil and BBB chain. On trailerable sailboats between 20 and 26 feet, which are relatively light to begin with, this formula works out to ⅜-inch line

(150 feet) and ³⁄₁₆-inch of chain (25-30 feet). This is a guideline and individual requirements may vary.

### Setting the Hook

Now that you have the perfect anchor and the perfect rode, you must have the boldness to set it right to make it work properly. A good bow roller that leads the rode fairly from the chock reduces friction, prevents gelcoat damage on deck and makes it easier to deploy and retrieve the anchor. It's also a good place to store an anchor and have it ready at a moment's notice. But all that is for naught if the procedure of anchoring remains a mystery.

The two most common mistakes are not paying out enough scope relative to the water's depth (a ratio of 7:1 is recommended) and backing down the vessel under engine too timidly. Scope is important because it reduces the pull-angle of the boat on the anchor, and the longer the rode, the more horizontal the pull.

Going in reverse with some juice is important to dig in the anchor. When you do that look around you as you go in reverse. Only when you are not moving relative to a fixed spot on shore or to other anchored boats nearby, the anchor is dug in. When you put the engine into neutral, you should notice a surge forward that's caused by the stretched nylon rode.

In crowded anchorages, you might not be able to pay out enough scope, because the room to swing at anchor is limited so you have to make up for that by a heavier ground tackle. Still, no sailor's life is complete if there hasn't been at least one anchor watch, sitting in the cockpit on a pitch-black night with the wind howling through the rigging, trying to guess if the other guys are moving up or if it's your anchor that slips. In most cases it'll be the latter.

Anchoring is a skill that must be practiced to develop mastery or at least confidence. There are several good how-to books available, which provide in-depth discussions of proper anchoring methods. It is a fundamental truth, however, that you will not be able to anchor with real confidence until you actually do it. So read up and go practice. Anchoring is one of the most important maneuvers for any sailor. Without exaggerating, it is essential to your enjoyment of the sport and to the safety of your vessel.

## ➤ BILGE PUMPS ◄

You have probably heard the old saying that nothing is as effective as a frightened sailor with a bucket in his hand. I strongly suspect that there is a great deal of truth to that statement. Yet, the truth is that hardly any boat has enough pump capacity on board to deal with water ingress caused by a damaged hull below the waterline. Standard bilge pumps are designed for the extraction of relatively small quantities of nuisance water caused by splash, spray, and seepage that is common to boats with wooden hulls.

Electric bilge pumps are great as long as they work. They can extract several hundreds to a couple of thousands of gallons per hour, and nobody breaks a sweat. What will happen, however, if the boat's electrical system goes down? A manual back-up pump will have to be manned. In this case, a sturdy and well-mounted manual diaphragm pump will be your best bet. Ergonomics are important because no pump can reach its capacity if the operator can't work it fast enough due to an awkward position in cramped quarters, or obstructions in the way of the handle.

The Whale Gusher 30 is an example for a dual-action pump with two diaphragms that is rated at 36 gallons per minute, provided there is enough elbow grease in supply. On the maintenance side it is necessary to pay attention to the flapper valves and the fit of the hose clamps. After use in saltwater, it is prudent to rinse a manual diaphragm pump with fresh water to prevent corrosion and salt build-up. The very least any small boat should have on board is one of the light and cheap manual piston pumps with an extended hose to discharge water from the bilge overboard.

Small electric bilge pumps for trailerable sailboats can be

had for less than $20, and are fairly easy to install. Debris strainers, hose, hose adapters, clamps and a mounting bracket will add to the initial purchase price, as will the float switch that triggers the pump if water in the bilge exceeds a certain height. Logic suggests that the intake of bilge pumps should be mounted as low as possible, and the hoses should be routed smoothly from the intake to the pump and from there to the discharge. If the water needs to be lifted out of a very deep bilge, install a corrugated intake hose and a smooth discharge hose. For ultimate safety, have a good-capacity water scoop on board in case the manual pump also fails. And forget the old adage about frightened sailors and buckets. A water scoop won't be enough to stop the boat from flooding in an emergency.

## ➤ EMERGENCY LIGHTS ◄

If you have a power outage that affects your navigation lights, U.S. Inland Navigation Rules permit the use of a light as a signal to other boats. As a precaution it is smart to have a good handheld Halogen lantern on the boat in case you need to make other boats aware of your presence. The rules require that the use of the light is such that it cannot be mistaken for one of your normal navigation lights, and that you do not use it in a manner that disrupts the navigation and safety of other vessels. In other words, don't shine a beacon into a wheelhouse, or into the eyes of another vessel operator who is at the helm of a passing boat.

## ➤ BINOCULARS ◄

A good pair of binoculars should be basic equipment on every cruising sailboat, regardless of size. It is an item that adds to the convenience and safety and often helps check the navigation for accuracy. Of course, you can break the bank buying a pair of image stabilizing binoculars. They are a dream because they compensate for vessel motion thus providing a stable view. But when they go overboard, get damaged or stolen, the pain is more than you might want to bear.

Instead, focus on a pair of unstabilized but waterproof 7X50 binoculars (7 is the power of magnification and 50 is the lens diameter) with Porro prisms that are made from BAK-4 glass for crisp, sharp images. The lenses should be filled with dry nitrogen to prevent fogging and offer a field of view of 350 feet or better at a distance of 1,000 feet. The light transmission should equal or exceed 90 percent for a bright image. An eye relief (the distance from the lens to the eye) of one inch is desirable if you wear glasses, so the eyes can discern the full field of view and a center focus wheel is preferable to the independent focus adjustments on the eyepieces. If they have flotation built into the housing, great, but a good neck lanyard should be enough to prevent them from going over the side.

Additional features like a rangefinder reticule to calculate the distance to an object of known height and a built-in bearing compass to determine the angle of your position relative to a known object are nice, but not essential and quite expensive. It might be better to have two sets of good binoculars on board for the price of one deluxe model.

## ➤ COMPASS ◄

A magnetic compass is essential on any boat, even a small dinghy or a kayak, let alone on a trailerable sailboat that is supposed to go places. It's a precision instrument that consists of a magnetic card that aligns with the earth's magnetic fields and points to the magnetic north pole. Ferrous metal in the vicinity of a compass wreaks havoc on the accuracy and should be avoided. If that isn't possible the compass' deviation must be adjusted (see below). The housing is filled with a clear, mineral oil that dampens the card's movement.

The vast majority of small-boat sailors will generally stay within sight of land, using a style of navigation that's called dead reckoning, i.e. steering by aids to navigation and landmarks that are marked on the chart and can be seen from the boat. Nevertheless, a compass is an essential instrument that helps you get home should the weather become foggy or otherwise deteriorate.

One Saturday morning at the sailing club, our Commodore told me about a 40-mile sail he had taken on his Catalina 22. Apparently, it was fantastic, broad reaching with fair winds. After he arrived at his destination at dusk, he had dropped the hook, had a good meal and spent a delightful night on the boat. The next morning when he raised his sails to return, a slight mist was in the air, which quickly developed into dense fog. The Commodore made it home safely because he had had the good sense to plot compass courses on the chart for the first leg of his sail. On his return trip, he ran the reciprocals (direct opposites) of his original compass courses to stay on a good return course.

There are a few things you should consider before buying a compass for your trailerable boat. Most likely you will settle for a magnetic compass, not for an expensive fluxgate model that contains electronics to compensate for local magnetic influence on the boat.

### Mounting Position

Probably the most important decision you have to make is where to mount the compass. This will dictate the style and size of your compass. I prefer a permanently mounted compass, but there are several alternatives for removable compasses that might be more suitable for your boat. The best spot on boats with wheel steering is the binnacle right in front of the wheel. That's where you'd want a compass, close to the helmsperson, centered with the longitudinal axis of the boat with good visibility. But few trailerable sailboats in our size range will have wheel steering, so a binnacle compass won't work. The alternatives are surface-mounted models that allow quick removal of the compass and are fairly easy to install. Flush-mounted deck compasses are another possibility, but they will require a cutout in the deck so they only leave the bubble visible. Bracket-mounted compasses can be adjusted to a variety of locations and angles and allow for easy removal and storage of the compass. Bulkhead-mounted models offer good visibility in the cockpit if mounted on the aft bulkhead of the cabin. Some racers mount them on one of the washboards that is inserted in the companionway so the crew can see it. When they don't need the instrument, it can be removed quickly. And if you want to go fancy, you can check out compasses or a combination of compass and other instruments that are mounted on the mast, below the boom.

### Card Types

Depending on your preference, you can choose between three different card types, the flat card, which is read from above and shows the entire compass rose, or the direct-read card that is read from the side. Some sailors find the latter easy to read, even though a direct-reading card is subject to more movement in rough conditions. The flat card displays the heading on the forward side of the card against a lubber line. The third card type is a hybrid between flat and direct cards, which offers the most versatility for reading a compass, e.g.on bulkhead models. Digital numeric displays are found on racing compasses and might take a little while to get used to. One step to make it easier is the use of numbers in combination with cardinal description (N, E, S, W, etc.)

### Size

Bigger is better, so get the largest size you can fit. Larger compasses are less affected by sudden and jerky motions. They also have larger course numbers, so they act smoother and they are much easier to read than small ones, especially in poor visibility.

### Deviation

If a compass does not point to the magnetic north, it most likely is influenced by ferrous metals in its vicinity such as a steering wheel, deck hardware, an engine etc. There are two ways to deal with this phenomenon: Find a less exposed mounting spot, or adjust the instrument to compensate for the deviation. A reasonably talented do-it-yourselfer who has read up on the process can take a stab at "swinging" the compass by moving the internal compensation magnets to correct the instrument. But there are also certified compass adjusters who will take care of this important task.

### Lubber Lines and Light

If the compass has to be read by the helmsperson from an angle, 45-degree and/or 90-degree lubber lines (in addition to the centered one) are very useful, eliminating the parallax error. If you plan on night sailing, make sure the compass has an internal illumination, so you won't have to turn on the flashlight and blind yourself and your crewmates every time you want to check your course.

### Bearing Compasses

Thus far we only discussed steering compasses that essentially tell you where you are going. But there is another type of compass that can be enormously useful, the hand bearing compass, because it helps measure the angle between the boat and another object on the water or ashore. Bearings taken of two or more objects with the compass are then transferred to the paper chart with so-called plot lines. The intersecting lines provide the position fix. Hand bearing compasses come with pistol grips or as "hockey pucks." Although GPS receivers can do the same and expensive binoculars have compasses built in, hand bearing compasses have a place on a small boat with limited electrical power.

It is a nautical truth that even a small sailboat is simply not properly equipped if it does not have a compass, because it would lack one of the most essential navigational tools. A good, permanently mounted compass costs anywhere between $70 and $300, depending upon the quality of the instrument, so even for budget-conscious sailors, there is no reason to leave the dock without one. Once you are ready to buy and install the compass, think about a plastic cover which protects it from sun, heat, rain and dirt when the boat is not in use.

## ➤ GLOBAL POSITIONING SYSTEM ◄

The Global Positioning System, once also known as NAVSTAR, is a satellite-based navigation system that was conceived and implemented by the U.S. military. As a side effect it has turned navigation for civilians around the world into a matter of pushing buttons and getting position fixes within seconds that are accurate to a distance of less than 10 feet. Nowadays GPS receivers are not just more accurate than they were five or ten years ago, but also less difficult to figure out, thanks to improvements to the user interface. Touch screens (in color, of course), voice prompts and digital speech interfaces that make the box talk back to you are now mainstream technology in GPS receivers, especially if they are used in cars. For the small-boat artist this may or may not be interesting since dual use is tempting, but only if the unit is waterproof and capable of taking the abuse on a trailerable boat, which includes bumps, drops, exposure to heat, saltwater and direct sunlight. In essence there are three different types of GPS receivers: handhelds, fixed-mount and portable fixed-mount that can easily be switched from the car to the boat. While handhelds draw power from AA batteries, which limits them somewhat, the latter two work around the clock, as long as they are hooked up to a 12V power connection.

### Electronic Charts

Electronic charts turn ordinary GPS receivers into chartplotters and handhelds into powerful and convenient navigation tools that follow their owners around from the car to the boat or anywhere else where a strong sense of position and direction might be desired. But there's a downside to it. It can be a bit confusing to find the right chart product for your GPS, because there are so many vendors and formats. Plus you can get the data either as a download from a CD or DVD via personal computer, which might require a digital passkey to unlock the information and usually requires a fee. Electronic maps and charts can also be pre-loaded into the receiver's internal memory by the manufacturer or it can be added via so-called cartridges that plug into a data port. Research that aspect before you acquire a GPS so you understand who supplies the maps and charts, how you get access to the data and how much it will cost you.

A popular bit of technology like a GPS receiver doesn't stay without company for long. On larger boats the GPS receivers/chartplotters can either be integrated in an on-board network of other instruments (radar and autopilot) or they have morphed into combinations that can also feature a VHF radio, a fishplotter or radar.

### What's Right for You?

The correct answer to this question depends on what style of boating you do and how much you want to rely on a piece of technology that is tremendously convenient and accurate, nearly foolproof, but not failproof. Your electrical system should be set up to handle on-board electronics if you like the idea of a fixed-mount GPS on your boat. If you are a bare-bones type, a handheld, battery-powered receiver will probably suffice, especially if you are inclined to use a GPS and a paper chart for course plotting. Alternatively, check out waterproof portable receivers that are nearly as easy to bring as handhelds and offer more advanced features and color screens that are nearly as large as those of fixed-mount GPS.

Several manufacturers like Garmin (www.garmin.com) or Lowrance (www.lowrance.com) or Raymarine (www.raymarine.com) offer compact and waterproof chartplotters with daylight-readable color screens that can be mounted in the companionway of a small trailerboat or even in the cockpit, where it can be seen from the helmsperson's position. Simultaneously, the battery-powered hand-held units have become smaller and smarter, with better color screens, integrated or downloadable digital cartography and the ability to create routes from the user's current position to the next waypoint. Longer battery life, more internal memory, built-in electronic compass, altimeter, location polling and, in some cases a built-in radio have nearly closed the gap to the low-end fixed chartplotters. A basic handheld receiver will start at about $150 and for sophisticated equipment the cost will go to $2,500 and beyond. A budget between $250 and 1,000 gets a very good handheld, portable or a compact fixed-mount GPS for your pocket cruiser.

### Accessories

What would life be without the add-ons and miscellaneous items that are necessary to get the best use of a newly purchased gadget like an iPod, a cell phone or a handheld GPS receiver? Here is a short list of GPS accessories: Cigarette lighter adapter for recharging, car kits, mounting brackets, external antennas, data cables and cartridges or a USB programmer to transfer map data from a map CD or DVD to the receiver's memory chip.

## ➢ PAPER CHARTS ≺

For several years now electronic and GPS chart plotters have been taking over the role that used to be held by paper charts for centuries. Even on commercial ships paper charts are going the way of the typewriter. But before we all become navigational couch potatoes there are a few more years left for printed charts, simply because it makes good sense and you can get them relatively cheaply. Sure, some trailer sailors won't bother with coastal navigation because they sail familiar venues and never venture far, but for those who intend to sail big, here are some thoughts about conventional paper charts.

- What is a nautical chart? If you have never seen one, think of it as a nautical map that shows features that are of particular interest to boaters like water depth, salient features on shore, potential hazards to navigation, and the location and types of aids to navigation. It is a primary tool to plan and plot courses and, like the manual bilge pump, a formidable backup when the ship's power is gone. Charts are marked with grids defined by lines of longitude and latitude, set off in degrees. The symbols are all explained on a separate chart, Chart No. 1.
- Who makes them? Because nautical charts are in the public domain, there are many vendors, but few go out and sound the ocean for charting purposes. Most countries with ocean access have an agency, office or institute that creates charts of the waters within their national boundaries. Charts of U.S. waters most likely are based on data that was collected and recorded by the National Oceanographic & Atmospheric Agency (NOAA), while Canadian charts come from the Canadian Hydrographic Service (CHS).
- What's the right scale? There is a simple rule: Large-scale charts (e.g. 1: 20,000) cover a small area in great detail. Small-scale charts (e.g. 1,00,000), cover a large area with little detail. Usually, you have a small-scale chart for the greater area you sail in and then a succession of larger-scaled ones (or a chart kit) that show sections of this area in greater detail.
- Waterproof or not? You want the detailed charts close to the helm and on a small boat that means they should be resistant to water and moisture. Unless you have a transparent protective sleeve for your charts, which is not all that cheap, buying waterproof charts on synthetic paper is a good idea.

They hold up for a long time, plus they are printed on both sides so they can save money in multiple ways.

- Should you use old charts? That's not a good idea, because hazards to navigation change, aids to navigation change, new piers and jetties are being constructed etc. Check the edition date at the bottom of the chart. If it is more than say three years old, think about getting a more recent edition.
- How to get the newest individual charts? West Marine offers a print-on-demand chart service with all the changes that reflect the latest Notice to Mariners issued by the Coast Guard. The caveat: They are not available in all but a few of their stores, so you need to call in your order and have them shipped to you, which adds time and money.
- What's the budget choice? If you have to watch your pennies and you can do without color, get Xeroxed black-and-white copies of the most recent editions of the charts you need.

Summarizing the rationale for having paper charts on board, despite GPS chart plotters and all the other electronics there are three reasons to go retro:

- You should have a backup to electronic navigation, especially on a small boat where power supply is very limited.
- Plotting your course on paper at the nav table while you are under way (and someone else is at the helm) is safe and sound practice.
- Any paper chart will beat the screen size, resolution and readability of a GPS monitor any time.

## ➢ EPIRBS ≺

We already observed that electronic emergency gear has shrunk in size while grown in features and Emergency Position-Indicating Radio Beacons (EPIRBs) are no different. It is a last-ditch, "help!-

come-and-get-me" device that is remarkably effective in saving lives—for a price. Whether a trailerable sailboat needs an EPIRB or the increasingly popular "EPIRB Light," the Personal Locator Beacon (PLB) depends on your style of sailing and, to a large degree, on your state of mind.

Here is the working principle of EPIRBs: When set off by contact with water they emit a coded distress call on radio frequencies that are reserved for distress signals, e.g. 406.028 and 121.5 MHz. Satellites pick up the ping and relay the information back to command centers from where rescuers in the vicinity of the incident are being sent out for a search-and-rescue mission.

An important distinction for EPIRBs is made by the way they are mounted on the boat, either with brackets that release the beacon automatically when the boat goes down or capsizes (Category I) and those that require manual release (Category II).

To speed up transmission and further boost the accuracy of the transmitted coordinates of the stricken vessel's position, EPIRBs can connect to a GPS receiver on board with a special cable or they have their own GPS transmitter built in. A position that's 100 yards accurate vs. 2 miles can make a big difference in time to rescue.

Many lives have been saved that way, but also many millions were wasted by false alerts, so there comes a responsibility with using an EPIRB. If you feel your kind of sailing is safer with an EPIRB on board, you will go out and buy one, but keep in mind that older units (121.5 Mhz) are being phased out and that many of the smaller, lighter and cheaper PLBs are not designed for marine use.

Modern EPIRBs transmit on the frequency of 406 MHZ and have distinct advantages over older models by offering better accuracy (2 nm vs. 12 nm) the possibility of transmitting an ID number so your boat's identity and itinerary can be quickly verified (only if the EPIRB was properly registered); they can store and rebroadcast the signal and their transmission power is much higher so they work better in adverse conditions, which most likely prevail when an EPIRB is being set off.

An EPIRB is a last-resort emergency communication equipment, and should be used only when lives are in immediate danger and there are no other ways to alert rescuers. EPIRBs were designed for blue-water sailing, far away from land. The same is true for the Personal Locator Beacons that are meant for people who pursue their thrills far away from civilization. I recommend you do some in-depth reading before you make a decision to buy an EPIRB for your boat.

## ➢ MISCELLANY ➤

Thus far we have covered a number of gear that qualifies as essential for sailing big on a small boat, or as a boost to safety. Before closing this chapter there are a few more items that deserve consideration.

### Radar Reflectors

They offer perhaps the best bang for the buck of all safety devices, next to PFDs, because they make your vessel visible in difficult conditions by enhancing the ability to reflect the energy of other vessels' radar beams. Sometimes, that difference can be a life insurance. Good solutions that won't eat up the cruising kitty are anodized aluminum reflectors that can be mounted under a spreader or high upon the backstay. Bigger cross sections are better, so go for the largest reflector that will reasonably fit. Mind the windage, though.

### Jackstays

Sailing shorthanded in rough waters, these lines are a great help to keep the crew on the boat, provided that the crew wears a safety harness with a tether to clip into a jackstay. Jackstays made of strong low-stretch line or polyester webbing can be rigged on centerline or on each side of the cabin from the cockpit to the bow and need to be attached at the strong points of the boat like the bow and stern cleats. An inflatable PFD with a built-in harness and a strong D-Ring for the tether is a simple and comfortable solution that eliminates the need for a separate safety harness.

### Throw Rope Bag

An item that has convinced sailors as a useful means to get a line to a person in the water or on a dock with accuracy on the first try is the throw rope bag. It consists of floating nylon line stuffed into a bag that is being thrown, while the bitter end is fastened to the boat or held in the idle hand of the pitcher. The best part about throw rope bags is that in a pinch you can make one yourself.

### Personal Safety Lights

If you do a lot of night sailing, you may want to consider keeping a couple of personal safety lights on board as accessories that can be clipped to a PFD or thrown to a person in the water. They can be incandescent, strobes or a combination of both. And they can guide rescuers to the victim from as far away as two miles.

## ➤ SUNGLASSES ◄

Remember, only you can take care of your eyes, so make certain you have a good pair of sunglasses for sailing. Sailing sunglasses should absorb 100% of UV A & B, and offer excellent infrared and blue light protection. Side shields or wrap-around designs that reduce lateral ambient light intrusion are pretty much a given now. Buying the right sunglasses won't be a cheap proposition, but they will be well worth the money. To make your investment last, get croakies that will tether the glasses around your neck. It isn't fun to see a $150 pair of shades sink in your wake.

Valentin Mankin, a very successful racing sailor and Olympic medalist from the former Soviet Union once said that he could see the wind in different colors on the water. With polarizing glasses you too will discover the different shades of wind, the puffs and lulls up ahead. They are a tremendous help to sail the boat more efficiently.

Beyond the obvious need to protect their eyes from UV rays, sailors constantly have to deal with glare that's created by the sun reflecting on the water, on white decks and hulls, windows and windshields, and on sails. Glare can badly affect your vision over the long run and such a condition wouldn't be conducive to sailing big, therefore invest in a pair of good shades and make sure you take precautions not to lose them.

## ➢ SAIL REPAIR AND RIGGING TAPE ≺

Rip-stop tape, as it is often called, is intended for emergency repairs for damaged sails. It sticks to fabric, is very strong and waterproof. If your sail rips, this stuff will reduce the probability that it will rip further and can save you repair money. These tapes are available in Dacron or Kevlar for jib and main and nylon for the spinnaker.

A practical cousin of the sail repair tape is the stretchy and self-bonding rigging tape that adheres only to itself, which makes it ideal for wrapping around turnbuckles or thimbles. They are inexpensive and don't add bulk, so there is no reason why you shouldn't have at least one roll on board.

## ➢ SUMMARY ≺

It is difficult to talk about safety or safety equipment without making some people feel a little nervous about undertaking an activity. I'm not sure that I can explain why this happens, but many people do have a tendency to get edgy, particularly when talking about safety on sailboats. Maybe it's because there has long been an air of adventure and mystery about sailing. Whatever the reason, I can assure you that ensuring safety on a trailerable sailboat is no more complicated than making certain your automobile will take you from one place to another safely. Hopefully, the tips and suggestions made in this chapter will give you a start.

# 7

# *The*
# *Amenities*

*To my mind the greatest joy in yachting is to cruise along some lovely coast, finding one's way into all sorts of out-of-the-way coves and rivers. A pleasant day's sail of four to six hours, and then, perhaps, a beat up some narrow, winding river.*

R.D. GRAHAM, Rough Passage

## ➤ INTRODUCTION ➤

Often when I anchor for the evening I want to escape from my everyday life. Sometimes the only thing I want to hear is the sound of silence. Sometimes I want to hear some good music. At other times I want to play cards or Trivial Pursuit with my family after a really good meal. Occasionally, I am on the water when my alma mater is playing an important football or basketball game, and I want to see it. I've found that a small portable television doesn't force the moon or stars to hide, the breeze to stop, or the birds to go away. I have one friend who reports watching his alma mater play football on television, while feeding the fish at the same time. Here are some suggestions that add to the comfort on a trailerable sailboat with the footnote that too much of a good thing will be too much. After all, stuff is fun to have but not all of it is really necessary, as it will add weight to the boat and influence performance and seaworthiness. So don't go into this like a kid into a candy store, but think carefully what makes the most sense for your style of sailing.

## ➤ SHOWERS ≺

After a long, hot day on the water a fresh-water shower is probably one of the more affordable luxuries that don't require a whole lot of technology to enjoy. If the trip ends at the dock in a well-equipped marina this will cost you a trip to the bathroom and a few quarters for hot water. Out in the wilderness, at anchor the story is different. The most logical and economical choice: the bucket. But wait, that's a waste of water if you have to get it from your on-board supply. On fresh-water venues, a bucket and some biodegradable soap like camp suds still are the simplest and environmentally most sensible choices, but what to do on the ocean?

You can have a shower that will lift your spirits and revitalize your energy, even if it's less than the experience in a four-star hotel. Outdoor and camping enthusiasts will be familiar with Sun Showers, which come in several different sizes, from 2.5 gallons, which is enough for two quickie showers, all the way up to 10 gallons.

Sun showers are nothing but a collapsible, "unbreakable" vinyl bag with a hose and a nozzle that's filled with water and is then set in the sun. One side of the bag is opaque with a black lining to absorb heat if it's laid out or hung up facing the sun, so the water is heated with clean and natural energy. When you are ready to take a shower, simply hang it up somewhere between the mast and the shrouds or hoist it with a spare halyard to a convenient height and you are in business. If you are concerned about privacy, get a vinyl enclosure. Also available is a powered model that plugs into the cigarette lighter. Either way, it is a cheap thrill and one that provides a most satisfying experience. Plus Sun Showers can be refilled and reused over and over again. It's a neat system and I recommend it. These are perhaps the best 30 dollars you can spend on sailing big.

## ➤ SCREENS ≺

I briefly mentioned the importance of hatch screens in Chapter 4 when we were discussing ventilation of the cabin. In many respects keeping bugs and insects away is never going to be a totally successful endeavor, regardless of the size of the boat. Like the elements of nature, insects give not one damn about your wealth, power, prestige, or the size and cost of your sailboat. It will certainly be more of a problem on larger boats with several hatches than it is on a typical trailerable sailboat. More openings offer more points of attack for the little critters that want to bite and annoy you.

The first line of defense is adding screens to your foredeck hatch and for the companionway, which production models of your trailerable sailboat most likely won't have. You can retrofit with pre-made screens or shade/screen combinations or, in the good old do-it-yourself tradition, you can fashion them yourself. Buy some mosquito netting from an army surplus or camping store, and cut it to fit your hatch opening. I sewed one side of some Velcro tape to the netting and outlined the hatch with the other side of the tape and some epoxy glue. The screen can be easily removed when I need to gain access to the foredeck through the hatch. You can make a similar screen for the companionway. Just be certain the screens attach from inside the cabin.

I really don't like to put on a lot of insect repellent, because I worry about the chemicals it contains. A viable alternative are Deet-free repellents, such as those offered for infants. But if that doesn't satisfy you, go on and protect yourself against pesky mosquitoes and no-see-ums. I recommend to spray some repellent around the edges of your screens. If you have a pop-top cover, by all means spray around the edges of the cover where it fits loosely. Take what precautions you can and know that those people on a 40-footer have a more difficult problem than you do. Good luck.

## ➤ BOARDING LADDERS ≺

Imagine a warm Saturday evening at your local sailing club. Three boats motor out to the middle of the moonlit lake and raft up. The one in the middle drops its anchor to keep the raft in place. Everyone puts on a swimsuit and jumps over the side. The lake is fed by a river and you can feel the cool stream of water as it moves past your body. Once you are sufficiently cooled off, you swim up to the boat to get back on board and, looking up, see that the top of the transom looks as high as the Queen Mary 2. How in the world are you going to pull yourself out of the water, over the side, and into the cockpit? No problem, you say. Well, if you haven't tried it you have no idea just how hard that act can be. This is particularly true for young children, and for older folks. And just to scare you some more, entire crews have succumbed to hypothermia after jumping over the side of a sailboat that drifted in a total calm in the middle of the ocean, just because nobody thought about a boarding ladder or at least dropping a line over the side.

Boarding or swim ladders, to be honest, should be listed as necessities, not just to climb back on board after taking a dip, but also to have a means of getting a crew back on board who went into the drink involuntarily. The issue is a bit less pressing on modern boats with built-in transom steps, but it is still a good idea to have at least a collapsible, removable ladder on board.

Swim ladders come in a wide variety of styles but there are a few design features to consider for usability and practicality, especially on a trailerable boat:

- Use ladders with hull stand-offs that provide more stability.
- There should be at least a couple of rungs extending down below the water surface, which makes it easier to get a foot on the bottom rung, to push the body's weight up, especially for a fully clothed person who fell in the water.
- The transom might not be the best spot for a ladder, be-

cause that's where the pitching motion of a boat is most pronounced. Often, ladders that can be hung over the side further forward are safer.

- Select a ladder that has flat, wide treads, not just round rungs that are painful to stand on.
- The last few inches are the hardest to conquer, so get a model that provides side rails that extend above deck.
- Light aluminum ladders with polyethylene steps are OK, but models made from stainless steel are more sturdy and better looking.
- On a small boat, storage is an issue, so consider a collapsible or telescoping model.

## ➤ MARINE BATTERIES ◄

To power your gadgets your boat will need batteries that provide the energy and can be recharged either by an alternator or via shore power. But batteries are heavy, so a small boat has limitations. In general, there are two purposes for batteries on a boat: One is cranking the starter of the engine, the second is to run your electrical equipment.

While we could go into a dissertation about battery chemistry, cranking amps, reserve minutes, discharge cycles and the virtue of having two separate batteries for these jobs, we probably should stick with the basics that apply to a trailerable boat, meaning that there will be only one battery that has to be able to do both. If the boat has an outboard engine with manual starter, there still has to be one house battery, if there is anything on board that requires electricity such as running and interior lights, a fixed VHF radio or GPS chart plotter or an electrical bilge pump. Look at deep-cycle batteries that have good storage and re-charging characteristics as an alternative to common lead-acid models. If you have an inboard engine with alternator choose a maintenance-free dual-purpose battery with gel or absorbed glass mats (AGM) technology. For a little more money they provide enough cranking power for the engine and they can be quickly recharged after being run down to a 10.5 volts. For best battery performance, stick to the following simple guidelines:

- Use smart charging that adjusts voltages to the ambient temperatures.
- Keep the battery cool, clean and dry.
- Check terminals for corrosion and clean it with a mix of baking soda and water to maintain conductivity.
- If you have more than one battery, use the same type of chemistry to avoid the complications of different charging techniques required by the different types of battery chemistry and don't mix old and new batteries in the same bank.

### ➤ SHORE POWER, CHARGERS AND INVERTERS ➤

For devices that consume a lot of energy, shore power is a godsend. Instead of draining the boat's batteries, they draw electricity from an outlet at the dock, which provides 125V AC power. You will need a power inlet mounted on the boat, usually on the side of the cabin or on the deck near the cabin. Once the power inlet is installed, wires of the proper gauge are run from the inlet to a household wall plug mounted inside the cabin. Use a 30 Amp cord and inlet on the boat because most marinas will supply this service. In case you end up in a marina with 15A or 20A service, a waterproof adapter is all you need.

The power inlet and associated parts are not expensive but don't scrounge on the installation. If possible, have your dealer or a certified marine electrician install it. The potential hazards from a poorly or incorrectly installed power inlet are too great a risk.

### Battery Chargers

The other benefit of shore power is the ability to charge your boat's battery, using a battery charger. Charging batteries is a complex topic and a potential source of confusion. If your boat is outfitted with one of these systems, make sure you understand the proper operation. If terms like charge curve, recovery time, equalization and acceptance phase sound Greek to you, don't despair. Consulting with experts or boning up on the topic with a good book (see recommendations below) will help you understand the basics of battery charging.

### Inverters

Now that we have gone over batteries and how to charge them, it seems only fair to talk about the inverter, that magic box that converts 12V or 24V DC power that comes from your boat's battery into 115V AC household current, which is needed by lights, appliances and laptop computers. Inverters are used to power appliances with a low electricity draw and can be combined with chargers in so-called charger/inverters. If you want to retrofit your trailerable sailboat with a charger or inverter, and you don't have a background as a marine electrician, you may want to resort to the same tactic as discussed above, i.e. talking to experts or studying some good literature.

I have not had a shore power connection on any of my previous sailboats. Instead, I made due with a 100-foot outside extension cord and ran it from the nearest power outlet to my boat. I would then plug in a two-socket adapter and could run whatever I thought I needed. My thinking about shore power was that if my 100-foot extension cord wasn't long enough to reach an outlet on shore, I defined my boat as "out to sea" and not in need of the power.

After years of winging it, I grew tired of having to look for a power outlet, running the extension cord back to the boat in a manner that would keep people from tripping over it, and having to find a place to store 100 feet of extension cord aboard when it was not in use. I became a convert and graduated from the extension cord to a shore-power connector. If you are in love with electrical and electronic gadgets, your boat probably needs one, too.

Marine electrics and electronics are a complex topic that deserves a much deeper discussion. If you are interested in more indepth information about the subject, look at these two titles by Sheridan House: *Understanding Boat Batteries and Battery Charging* and *The Marine Electrical and Electronics Bible* both by John C. Payne.

## ➤ CLEAN POWER ≺

With fossil fuels (and electricity generated by fossil fuels) getting a bad rap, the demand for renewable energy like solar or wind power is on the rise. Sailors can take advantage of both by using photovoltaic solar panels and wind generators. Besides, renewable energy is more than clean. It's also a ticket to more independence if you plan to be away from shore for a while.

Both technologies have been around for years and great strides were made to improve their efficiency, on wind generators probably more than on solar panels. Large wind turbines have become an important source for the energy supply in many countries around the world and photovoltaic cells now can be integrated in roof shingles or even house paint. But while progress was made with solar and wind power technology, they might not (yet) be suitable as primary energy sources, but at the very least, they are great to supplement your energy household.

### Solar Panels

Solar panels use the photovoltaic process to create electrical current through silicon wafers that are exposed to sunlight. Unlike generators or auxiliary diesel engines with alternators, they are quiet, simple, clean, and practically free of maintenance, which is not to be discounted when looking for ways to generate electricity.

Multiple cells are coupled to form modules that produce DC power. Output (or amperage) depends on the size and efficiency of the cells and the intensity, duration and angle of the sunlight. Multi-crystalline panels are more efficient than amorphous silicone panels, as long as the exposure to sunlight is strong. However, they are less productive in diffused light or when some of the modules are partially shaded. Silicon panels with their smaller output are a good choice to provide power to trickle charge a battery when the boat is not in use. They can be small to fit the limited deck space on a trailerable sailboat or stuck under a deck hatch with suction-cup mounts.

The demand for solar panels has grown exponentially with no end of the boom in sight, but realistic expectations are in order, especially if direct sunlight is in short supply. If you live in California or Arizona, you will get more miles out of solar technology, simply because more direct sunlight is available. But that's not the whole story, because solar panels don't like heat, which causes them to lose efficiency. A clear, cold winter day with bright sunlight produces the highest peak output, but the fact that on such a day the sun angle is likely to be low and the period of direct sunlight is short, limits a panel's output. Panels that produce less than 1.5 percent of your battery system's rated capacity usually don't require a regulator.

Getting the right size for a photovoltaic solar system on your boat—preferably in amps to compare a solar system to an alternator or charger's rating—is a matter of solving the equation Amps=Watts/Volts. Do that for each device the solar panel is supposed to power and estimate how long the device is being run on a weekly or monthly basis and you have a rough outline of your electrical budget. Whether you believe the inconvenient truth of global warming or simply feel the sting of high prices at the pump, a solar panel might be in your boating future.

### Wind Generators

Another way to generate electricity for your on-board needs of DC current is the wind generator. Look around in any anchorage and you will find that the saltiest-looking boats probably have some sort of wind generator that stoically whirrs in the breeze. If you have been to Northern Europe, or seen the forest of windmills while slogging through a commute over Altamont Pass in the greater San Francisco Bay Area, you know that power generation with the help of wind is more than a fad.

For a small wind generator on a sailboat the key is being able to maintain efficiency with the constantly changing wind speeds. The better ones have microprocessor controls to regulate rpms and the rate of charge that goes to the battery.

But too much of a good thing can indeed be too much, at least for a run-of-the-mill wind generator. If the breeze pipes up beyond 30 knots, older or low-end models have to be tethered, turned away from the breeze, slowed or stalled somehow to prevent over-heating and overcharging. Invest in a good wind generator and see what it can do in conjunction with solar panels to make you independent of fossil fuel. Wind as a renewable source of energy has a big advantage over solar, because it can blow at night too.

## ➤ AUTOPILOTS ≺

An autopilot is an electromechanical steering device that holds a sailboat on a compass heading that you set for it. If you have ever sailed in open water for several hours, you know how tiring long periods of time at the tiller can be, not to mention the problem of boredom and wandering attention. Relief from the tedium of extended periods at the tiller is one of the real benefits of an autopilot.

Even if you haven't sailed for hours on open water, you have most likely thought you were steering a straight course, only to look at your wake and discover just how crooked a course you actually did steer. An autopilot actually steers a straighter course than you can. In doing so it can reduce both the distance and the time sailed to your destination.

With few exceptions, small trailerable sailboats, if they can accommodate an autopilot at all, will have tiller steering that requires a linear push-pull model. Don't assume the manufacturer's recommendations are necessarily right for your boat without making sure that the unit can handle the helm forces. To get an idea how much force such a gadget has to cope with, grab the tiller one foot forward of the rudderpost where an autopilot would be mounted and see how hard it is to steer the boat precisely.

Check how many degrees per second the unit can correct and think about the power draw (approx. 0.5 amps in standby mode, 1.5 in use) and how you account for that consumption with your electrical system.

Network and software technology taught autopilots how to talk and listen to other on-board instruments like GPS or wind instruments. This enables them to respond to heading errors relative to the next waypoint, changing conditions like more wind and the resulting stronger weather helm, or a change in apparent wind direction relayed by the electronic wind indicator at the tip of the mast. All cool stuff, but you decide if it has a place and a budget on a small trailerable sailboat.

Autopilots are expensive. Even for smaller sailboats they cost anywhere between $400 and $1000 and that does not include extras or installation. My advice is to consider the sort of sailing you will normally be doing. If most of your sailing involves short distances, an autopilot may be too costly for the return in comfort it provides. On the other hand, if you will be involved in sailing that requires several continuous hours at the tiller, an autopilot may be just the ticket. It will certainly make your small sailboat bigger.

Despite all their abilities, there are two things autopilots aren't good at: Anticipating the moves of other vessels nearby and reacting to other vessel traffic. Until the unit is deactivated or adjusted (either manually or by an electronic instrument it is connected to) it will steer the course it was set for, so the crew must keep a sharp lookout. It is not smart to set it and forget it, possibly going below for an extended period of time. Doing so is simply inviting trouble.

## ➢ WIND INDICATORS ≺

There is a difference between true and apparent wind direction. If you are standing on a dock with the wind directly on your right cheek, you are feeling the direction of the "true" wind at that spot. If you start walking, you will feel the wind shift slightly forward on your face. Now you're feeling the "apparent" wind, which is a combination of the true wind and the headwind you are creating by walking forward. In the same way, if you are sailing with the true wind directly across your starboard beam, the forward movement of the boat will shift the apparent wind forward. Just how far depends on the speed of the true wind and the speed of your sailboat. The essence of sailing is to know the direction of the apparent wind, so there are several simple ways that help gauge where it's coming from.

### Windex

The most effective is a little arrow-like device located on top of the mast, called a masthead fly, or by a popular product name, Windex. While the boat is sitting motionless at the dock, the masthead fly will point in the direction of the true wind; once the boat is moving it points into the direction of the apparent wind and you use it to trim the sails accordingly. A mechanical Windex is inexpensive and easy to install. There are electronic versions too, but unless you are using wind instruments for racing or long-distance cruising, they might be overkill on a trailerable boat.

### Telltales

Telltales help you determine the apparent wind and/or the airflow over your sails, depending on where they are installed. Some telltales are attached to the shrouds, using a rotating plastic disc to allow them to turn in the wind. Old audiotape is a popular solution for the budget-conscious sailor. Like a masthead fly, telltales show the direction of the apparent wind and have some use in very light air when the Windex at the mast top is picking up a different breeze or nothing at all. A second type of telltale attaches to the sail with a sticky patch. It's a trick that was gleaned from glider planes that indicates how the air is flowing across the sails and helps maintain the best sail shape for the course, or sail the course that corresponds best to the sail trim. Telltales also can be found at the leech (aft edge) of the mainsail, showing how smoothly the flow of air comes off the sail, or whether the twist is correct. For the amount of valuable information they provide, telltales are a real bargain.

## ➢ GRABRAILS ➤

If your sailboat doesn't have teak grabrails (handrails), I strongly recommend you have them installed. This is particularly true if your boat has a traditional trunk cabin and you will be walking on the deck area between the side of the cabin and the gunwales. Grabrails are useful even when the boat is sitting in a slip, tied to a mooring, or at anchor because they provide a fixed spot to hold on to when stepping aboard or moving around on a fairly unstable surface. For example, stepping from a fixed dock onto the gunwale of the boat that is tied up alongside, you will immediately notice how the boat responds to your weight by heeling toward you and moving away from the dock. When you are under way and want to go forward around the cabin, there's absolutely no discussion about the safety value of handrails on the cabin top.

My advice is to install handrails that cover the length of the cabin roof, or at least in the logical spots where you need something to hold on, but where the rails won't interfere with deck hardware such as turning blocks cleats, winches or control lines. This is different on each boat and might require some thinking and a few trial runs, if the boat doesn't have this accessory installed at the factory. The best material for handrails depends on your personal taste and your willingness to maintain them. Modern boats will have stainless-steel rails, while you'll find teak rails on more traditional models.

Traditionalists claim there is nothing better looking than well-cared-for teak on the exterior of a sailboat. But a critical look around the marinas and the storage lots proves that this isn't true for the thousands of boats that suffer from neglect. Depending on the exposure of your boat to the elements and if you store it with a cover, teak handrails are one item on your spring project list that requires cleaner, brightener, sealer, and varnish or oil to restore their original luster. However, when they are finished, they will look so good you will get compliments from other sailors.

More important is the proper backing of the rails below deck, so they can withstand the weight of a grown up holding on, and possibly the shock load of someone falling and being held aboard by the tether of a safety harness that's clipped to the rails. Use sturdy backing hardware and stainless-steel bolts and make sure you seal the boltholes to prevent water from seeping into the laminate where the handrails are attached.

## ➢ BOAT HOOKS ➣

No sailboat is equipped to sail big without a boat hook. I know from experience that halyards can work loose and fly up the mast and/or wrap themselves around stays, usually four to six feet beyond the reach of a fully extended human arm. Boat hooks are useful for retrieving wayward halyards, snaring dock lines, or picking up the mooring. My advice is to buy a telescoping hook, one that expands to a minimum of six feet and has flotation built in, so there is a chance to get it back if it takes a swim. They don't cost much, won't take up much room on the boat, and will save you a lot of frustration and embarrassment in front of other sailors.

## ➢ DEPTH SOUNDERS AND SPEEDOMETERS ➣

The boat's speed through the water and the depth under its keel are two vital pieces of information a prudent mariner needs for safe navigation, even if he is blessed with a trailerable sailboat that has a swing keel or a centerboard that can be fully retracted, for maneuvering in very shallow water. It is true that these appendages minimize the danger of running aground, and make it easy to get under way again if you get stuck on a sandbank while folks on large keelboats might have to call for help to get out of the same predicament. But it is also true that even with a swing keel, nothing good comes from hitting "hard water," so unless you want to learn how to "swing the lead" or "sound it out" the old-fashioned way, a depth sounder/speedometer might be worth considering.

In principle, depth sounders do the same as ancient lead lines, but they use a transducer that sends out sound waves that bounce back from the bottom and are picked up again by the transducer. The time between sending the original ping and picking up the echo determines the water's depth. However, depth sounders are rarely a single instrument. Either they are combined with a speed log, which is very common on many small boats, or they have morphed into fishfinders, which have the capability to graphically display an exact representation of the bottom contours and the fish that might swim between the boat and that bottom. Either way, the principle is the same and both instruments are very useful for accurate navigation.

If you are planning to fish from your boat, consider buying a fishfinder, but be prepared for some research. Today's top-models with integrated GPS chart plotter go for $1,000 or more and can include features such as forward-scanning sonar that shows the bottom ahead of the boat's bow and can be useful for navigating, not just for fishing.

For our intents and purposes however, a simple combo of speedometer and depth sounder will do, with a digital LCD display that shows both numbers, which can be configured as primary and secondary by the user. Mounted at the rear bulkhead of the cabin this instrument is easy to see for the crew and the skipper and should be backlit for nighttime operation.

Other useful features, which are standard on most models, are configurable shallow-water alarm and keel offset, a function that tells the instrument to measure the depth from the bottom of the keel rather than the hull. That's important for boats with a fixed keel. If your vessel doesn't have one, make sure the depth sounder will measure and report very shallow depths of two feet or less without going crazy.

The speedometer should provide current speed, distance and trip data, which give the skipper or navigator an idea how the boat is performing through the water. If compared to the information from the GPS, which measures speed and distance over ground, important conclusions about the prevailing conditions can be made, e.g. whether the boat is sailing in adverse or favorable current, etc.

Now for the tricky part: Both functions need transducers to collect the data that's being displayed by the command unit. Sonar transducers for depth sounders need to be mounted where they are not disturbed by turbulent water and paddlewheel transducers for the speedometer must accurately measure the speed of the water as it rushes by the hull. The harsh reality is that most likely you will end up drilling a sizeable hole in the bottom of your boat's hull for both, preferably forward of the keel. The sonar transducer must point straight down to be accurate, while the paddlewheel only needs to be mounted somewhere near the center line where it will be submerged at all times, not lifted out of the water by heel.

The sailing venue, too, determines what kind of sonar transducer is appropriate. For deep-water sailing you'll need a transducer that can look far with a narrow beam width. In shallow lakes or estuaries, one that looks forward and to the side with a wide beam is more valuable. Make sure you get the transducers for your instruments that are recommended by their respective manufacturers.

If you have a phobia of drilling holes in the hull below the waterline, you might want to check out a portable depth sounder or models with a glue-in type transducer which are in use on personal water craft that allegedly can provide accurate soundings by "shooting" through solid fiberglass hulls.

If all that sounds like work, well it is, but it's time well spent because a depth sounder and a speedometer are useful instruments, not just in unfamiliar waters. They are indispensable for safe and accurate navigation in bays, sloughs, rivers, and lakes that trailerable sailboats frequently use and are often poorly marked by aids to navigation. Installing them is not just a step to sailing big, but also to sailing safely.

## ➤ SAIL AND BOAT COVERS ≺

Your sails are your boat's engine so you should take care of them. Non-sailors love sail covers because they make a sailboat look neat and tidy. While they may achieve that, their primary purpose is to protect your sails from the destructive effects of the sun and the weather. An uncovered mainsail furled on the boom, allowed to bake in the sun, flap in the wind, and broil in the humidity will soon suffer from a breakdown of the cloth's fibers. This is also true of the jib. Furling jibs can have covers, too, but mostly they only use colored sailcloth at the leech that is extra-UV resistant, so when the sail is rolled up entirely, only this colored leech cloth shows. Also, don't forget that water or at least dampness can accumulate under the cover after some rain, so a cover from breathable fabric sounds like a good idea.

A lot can be said about materials, but it all comes down to the simple truth that you get what you pay for. Cotton is cheap but won't last. Vinyl is tough, but not the most fashionable choice and hard to handle when it's cold. Solution-dyed polyester that's covered with urethane is a good compromise, water repellent, strong, breathable, UV and stretch resistant and relatively affordable. A popular choice is Sunbrella, which has become the de-facto standard for breathable boat and sail covers. If it doesn't clash with your sense of style, choose dark colors like black, dark blue or green because they contain more dye, which makes the covers more UV resistant. The closures can be hook-and-loop, metal slugs, or plastic zipper, which sooner or later will become a source of trouble.

Sail covers are not really an amenity, but a necessity if you want to protect your investment. You should also get a cover for your wooden tiller so you won't have to clean, sand, brighten, and varnish the tiller every season.

For the same reason you should consider a full cover for storing your boat, simply because it will keep dirt, water and vermin out, protect the lines and hardware from aging prematurely in the sun, and prevent gelcoat oxidation, which gives older boats that neglected look. Here too, breathable fabrics are preferable over budget solutions. If you are in the habit of going on the road frequently, you might have to invest in a cover that is specially built for trailering, with double-folded hems, four-ply seams and reinforcements in high-wear areas and, of course, sturdy, sewn-in loops for tie-downs to prevent the cover from flapping in the breeze.

Before you go on the Internet to find custom cover shops (there are many), check with the manufacturer of your little yacht if sail and boat covers are offered as an accessory.

## ➤ ENTERTAINMENT ELECTRONICS ≺

I had been daysailing in the Gulf of Mexico, just off Gulf Shores, Alabama, and was heading back through a small inlet to the Intracoastal Waterway, just as the tide had reached its strongest outflow. The winds and tide combined to create a really volatile sea. So after dropping the sails and starting the outboard, I sent my nephew below to turn on the stereo, jack up the volume and put Wagner on the cassette player. We forged ahead accompanied by the strains of Wagner's music, rising and falling to the crashing of the boat in the choppy seas. It was quite a ride.

And after an exciting passage, music continues to be a great companion aboard, but I had no idea of the serenity and peace it can contribute to life until I had anchored in a quiet bay and listened. At night, after the breeze has settled down and the sea becomes placid, I could hear notes and riffs I missed when ashore.

Music is still music, but technological evolution has spawned pocket-sized gadgets such as the immensely popular MP3 players, satellite radios and portable DVD players that make it easier than ever to turn a cozy cabin into a floating home entertainment center. In essence, digitally recorded audio and video is rapidly replacing the clutter of cassette and videotapes or compact discs. To whet your appetite, here are some options:

### Receivers and CD Players

Despite all the new gadgets, for most of us, the most common way to listen to music on a sailboat is a stereo receiver that offers AM/FM radio, plus a tape or compact disc player. The cassette option is outdated, but if your boat was previously owned by someone else, it still might be there. And that isn't bad, because with a car connecting pack that's available for a few dollars at any electronics store, external devices such as iPods or portable CD players can be played back through the tape. If the receiver is new, it probably will have a built-in CD player that can play normal music CDs with up to 70 minutes of content or CDs that were ripped from digital MP3 audio files on a computer and offer several hours of music.

To take advantage of your iPod's music library on a modern stereo that doesn't have a cassette player, you might need a Y-adapter audio cable that connects devices with a 3.5 mm audio jack to RCA input plugs. Apple will be expensive, but generic cables that work just as well can be found for less than $10.

The key is to install a *marinized* receiver (not a car stereo!), which means that the unit is specially prepped, e.g. the electronic circuits are coated with resin so they withstand heat, humidity and salty air. Costs a bit more but years of trouble-free use should be worth it.

Another way to approach on-board music entertainment is looking at portable music systems, aka boom boxes that include satellite speakers and a sub-woofer. If that option sounds appealing, choose a model that can operate on 12V DC and 110V AC. The better ones offer a way to connect external devices such as music players or short-wave radios with an adapter cable.

### Speakers

Often music is better when enjoyed in company, so it needs to be piped through good speakers that are properly mounted, i.e. pointing toward the listener. On a small boat the choices for mounting cockpit speakers are limited and producing good sound is much more challenging than in a car that can be closed off.

The first decision to make is whether you go for flush-mounted speakers that take advantage of enclosed space behind them (e.g. a lazarette) to produce decent bass response or box speakers that can be installed anywhere but might be a bit bass-challenged. Like receivers, speakers should be built explicitly for marine use with non-corroding metals and magnetic shielding to prevent interference with on-board instruments. Take care to choose the correct size speakers that can handle the output of the stereo amplifier. Look for unstranded 18-gauge wire with sealed ends to connect speakers and stereo and make sure you connect the positive terminals of the speakers to those on the amp.

### Accessories

A waterproof remote control, although less of an issue on a small boat, can be quite practical to adjust the sound and volume of the stereo without having to get up and crawl down below to where the receiver most likely is mounted. If the stereo lives in the cockpit, or if cutting an opening into a bulkhead is not an option, a gimbal mount (with or without splash cover) is the alternative. And lastly, a few dollars invested in an external AM/FM radio antenna might make the difference between annoying static noise and hearing the powerful brass section in Beethoven's Fifth Symphony.

### Satellite Radio

Designed for the automotive market, satellite radio quickly found a following with boaters. In a nutshell, the radio signal is broadcast from the studios to your receiver via satellite. At this writing, two services, XM Radio (www.xmradio.com) and Sirius (www.sirius.com), with more than 100 commercial-free channels each are vying for listeners in the U.S. The difference between both is largely subjective (depending if you are a football or baseball fan), except that Sirius is using orbiting satellites while XM relies on stationary ones. Both services require special receivers and charge set-up and monthly subscription fees. Here are several reasons for satellite radio's appeal:

- Clarity: No static or other distortion to impede the signal. Quality rivals CD or MP3 digital sound.
- Coverage: Both systems provide continuous coverage across the continental US and up to 200 miles offshore, way more than you'd be able to get with terrestrial AM/FM radio transmissions.
- Do you realize the joy of listening to radio that's commercial free?
- Comfort: Satellite radio is the younger, more talented cousin of analog AM/FM radio. The receiver displays the name of the artist, song title, channel name and number, much like satellite TV.
- Variety: 100 channels (60 music, 40 for news, talk, sports and entertainment) are divided into blocks of channel numbers. Available music categories include genres like pop, rock, hip-hop, classic, jazz, dance, R & B or country.
- Portability: A plug-in receiver follows you from your boat to your car and into your home. Combined with an FM modulator, satellite receivers connect to existing stereos albeit at a lower sound quality (comparable to what you'd get on FM radio).
- Online access: Subscribers to the Sirius service get free online access to stream the programs to their computer as well.

All in all, from trailer boating in rural areas to coastal and offshore cruising, satellite radio suits many different tastes and boating styles.

### Television

Watching the tube is the prototypical couch-potato sport, remote in hand and surfing channels. But that's changing too, since catching the most favorite programs no longer requires viewers to be near a set at a certain time or even near a TV at all. Recording

technologies such as TiVo that can be programmed with some so-
phistication made TV independent of programming times.
Portable gadgets like video iPods (and soon also cell phones)
allow viewers to download their favorite shows via the Internet
and take them on the road or on the water to watch them whenever
and wherever they please. So even if you miss your Alma Mater
play the game of the year, there are means to catch the action.

Still, some love the idea of vegging out in front of the TV on
their boat. A small trailerable boat will probably force you to consider a small portable TV, rather than a lavish HDTV-ready 26"
flat-screen model that's mounted on the main bulkhead in the
cabin. Like a portable stereo, a boat TV benefits from dual voltage
compatibility, operating on 12V DC through an adapter that plugs
into a cigarette lighter or 110V AC if your boat is setup with an inverter. These TVs are quite common not just for marine use, but
also with snowbirds, who are cruising the country in recreational
vehicles.

But installing the TV and ensuring it has enough juice (if it
doesn't run on battery power) is only the first part of the exercise.
To get a decent signal you need a separate antenna, which can pick
up VHF, UHF and FM frequencies. The smallest ones weigh less
than 10 ounces and can be mounted on the mast. To make your
radio work with a TV antenna you need an AM/FM/TV splitter.

## ➤ FLAGS AND FLAGSTAFFS ➤

I think that a sailboat flying a U.S. Yacht Ensign, or other "dressy"
flags looks neat and nautical. Flagstaffs should be of a certain size
and match your boat's proportions. Choose an ensign that is one
inch long for every foot of boat length, which means that a 24-
footer should have an ensign that's two feet long. The flagstaff
should have twice the length of the ensign's vertical side and be
mounted on the transom or sternrail. They are not expensive and
are a nice and simple way to dress your boat. Refer to *Chapman*

*Piloting* for a good discussion of recommended flag size and proper etiquette for displaying flags.

## ➤ SUMMARY ≺

Some years ago I would walk the docks and stop almost exclusively at sailboats in the 35- to 45-foot range. I would walk right past the smaller boats, guided by the mistaken assumption that the owners of the larger sailboats sailed more frequently, and in more comfort than the people on the smaller sailboats. For some reason, I believed that only "large" could mean comfort and convenience. I was fundamentally wrong. I didn't know then what I know now, that given the right gear and equipment, you can sail big on a small sailboat.

Still, at the end of this chapter it is time to remind you that festooning a small boat with a lot of gear and supporting systems is a two-edged sword. While it might increase convenience and creature comfort, it also will weigh down the boat, which means it won't sail at peak performance, especially not in light air and it will alter its behavior in a seaway. Don't rush in and go on an indiscriminate shopping spree. Take it easy, go sailing and take notes. Be judicious about adding gear and make sure it doesn't just increase the displacement of your vessel but also your enjoyment of the sport and the little yacht's safety and seaworthiness. And don't forget those drink holders you can clip to the lifelines. They are worth their weight in gold.

# 8

# Buying Used: Sailing Big and Saving Big

*Cast out into the world of truth and co*
*the real search began. No longer was our*
*"what do you want in a boat?" Now it w*
*do you refuse to do without?" The list oɟ ʋur re-*
*quirements shrank to one-third its former length,*
*and even those items were shuffled, reconsidered,*
*and modified. Boats we would not even have looked*
*at before were now seriously considered. But the*
*sunset we were going to float off into had lost none*
*of its allure. Only the floater had changed . . .*

HERB PAYSON, Blown Away

## ➤ INTRODUCTION ≺

There are a lot of people who are put off by the idea of buying anything, a car, a boat or an RV, if it isn't brand new. Then there are
many who simply can't afford to buy those things unless they are
used. But there are also sly and patient customers, who want to buy,
but who are perfectly happy to save their own money and allow others to watch the depreciation of a new car or boat. If you fall into
one of the latter two categories, this chapter is written for you. Judg-
ing by the fact that the vast majority of boats bought and sold in the
U.S. are used, this theory is built on solid economic foundation.

If I had insisted on buying only new sailboats, my sailing
days would have been delayed by at least 25 years. The fact is
that I have never owned a brand new trailerable sailboat. At first
I couldn't afford to; later on I didn't want to. Even though I have
never had a new sailboat, I have had very fine, well-equipped
trailerables that I have sailed happily and frequently because I

aid attention to six factors: availability, affordability, liveability, sailability, raceability, and cruisability.

A few manufacturers such as W.D. Schock, Hunter Marine, MacGregor, and Catalina Yachts have combined to produce tens of thousands of trailerable sailboats in the 22- to 26-foot range. This means that there is a lively and competitive used-boat market, which is good for potential buyers. Like automobiles, sailboats depreciate in value, some more than others. Unlike cars, trucks, and vans however, most sailboats are not used on a daily basis and do not take the beating that urban and suburban driving exerts on vehicles. As a result, a well-maintained fiberglass sailboat has a much longer life expectancy than a comparably maintained road vehicle. I'm not trying to say that trailerable sailboats are not subject to wear and tear, because that simply isn't true. But in contrast to the days of wooden boats, modern composite building materials such as fiberglass laminates tend to have a much longer life.

Another great advantage is the use of the Internet to do some windowshopping and virtual fender kicking. Comparing prices and equipment from the comfort of your desktop flattens the learning curve tremendously and helps educate potential buyers. Web sites such as www.boats.com or the brokerage site www.yachtworld.com provide algorithms to define the search criteria and good returns. More on that later, but if you are cautious and diligent, you can do your homework on the Net before you go out and buy a used trailerable sailboat with confidence.

The real bonus of buying a pre-owned boat is that you can buy a used trailerable sailboat that is well equipped for a lot less than a new boat of the same size and make that is bare bones. Boats depreciate most during the first two years. Here are some examples showing the initial savings when buying a used boat. Many years ago I bought a used 1977 Catalina 22 for $4,000. The boat, which was nine years old, was in excellent condition. A new Catalina 22 would have cost three times as much at the time, an immense savings. But it didn't stop there because my used sailboat came with the following equipment that wasn't standard with a new boat:

1. A trailer
2. A boom vang
3. A VHF radio and mast mounted antenna
4. A 7 h.p. outboard motor with gas tank and bulb line
5. A porta-potti
6. A two-burner stove
7. A mainsail cover
8. A tiller cover
9. Sailbags
10. Four PFDs
11. Cockpit cushions
12. Flare gun and flares
13. A paddle
14. Three fenders
15. A clinometer
16. A Windex
17. A tiller tamer
18. New interior carpet
19. Cabin curtains
20. Reupholstered cabin cushions
21. A fire extinguisher

If you take this list of equipment and calculate replacement costs, it would have cost more than the entire used boat. Even if we assume that the equipment's replacement value was only 50 percent because it was used, too, that still made a big difference. Adding up the savings for the accessories and what I saved by buying a used vessel, the total nearly equaled what a new un-equipped Catalina 22 would have cost at the time.

> MATTERS OF THE CHECKBOOK ≺

OK, you have decided that you want to go sailing, and you are going to do it the only way you can—on an affordable, used 22- to 26-foot trailerable sailboat. Now it is time for one of your tougher decisions. How much money can you afford to spend on a used boat? Be certain that you decide how much you are able to spend, and not how much you want to spend. If you are careful and keep this distinction in mind, you will find that you own the boat, rather than the boat payments own you.

Take a long, hard, and realistic look at your budget. You already know if your budget will not stand the expense associated with buying a new trailerable sailboat, not to mention the additional cost associated with equipping it. You need to do the numbers to figure out precisely how much money you can invest in the acquisition of a vessel and how much budget you have to cover the operating cost. If you have $10,000 to play with and don't want to pay cash for your purchase, check with your lending institution to find out how much is required for a down payment and how the monthly payments add up each year. You may find that a used trailerable boat that costs $10,000 requires a down payment of 20 percent, or $2,000, and an additional $4,000 in monthly payments. So for $6,000 you will buy the right to use the boat for the first year, while it will take several more years until the loan is paid off before that expense goes away, you get the title and become the rightful owner. This example will leave you with 4,000 dollars, part of which you may use to cover taxes, restoration, replacements, registration of vessel and trailer etc., so you can use the boat the way you want to.

Calculate a separate monthly operating budget that consists of fixed and variable costs, such as storage, insurance, miscellaneous maintenance, gas, oil, and travel money, because you have a boat on a trailer that can go places. Considering the hourly rates for boatyard, do-it-yourself ingenuity can cut down on maintenance and restoration cost, but you still are on the hook for the fixed expenses.

If there is any consolation, remember, you will have finished paying for your used sailboat long before the person making payments on a new boat that costs three to five times as much. Paying a fair price and getting a good boat in return is essential to being happy with your used trailerable sailboat, so here are a few suggestions for starting your research.

## ➤ HOW TO FIND GOOD USED BOATS ≺

I have a friend who once owned a Catalina 22 which he had, over the years, equipped to sail really big. My friend kept the boat at a sailing club on a lake only twelve miles from his home, and quite often he would go daysailing or spend a weekend on the boat. In addition, two or three times a year he would load it on the trailer, drive to the coast, and go on three- or four-day cruises with his wife and daughter.

Unfortunately, the "bigger is better" bug bit him and he bought a 30-foot, fixed keel sailboat. He had to sell his well-equipped Catalina 22 so he could afford to buy his new 30-footer that he sails maybe three or four times a year. The rest of the year he is privileged to pay hundreds of dollars a month for a deep slip in which to keep his "bigger and better" boat. Not to mention yard bills for haul-outs and bottom jobs. Now he still drives the 12 miles out to the lake, but to watch the trailerable sailboats go sailing in the warm breezes of a sunny day. And when he gets around to sailing his 30-footer, his friends often tow their trailerable sailboats to the coast, and go sailing with him. Viewed from this perspective, getting rid of his trusted trailerable sailboat doesn't look like such a smart move. But take heart, because my friend's decision (and that of others like him) to "move up" to a bigger boat is the gain for people who want to buy a good used trailerable sailboat.

### Regular Sources

Like my friend with the Catalina 22, a lot of sailors sell their smaller boats for a bigger one, and by doing so put a lot of good used trailerable sailboats on the market. For a potential buyer, the objective is to gather as much information as possible, either the old-fashioned way by reading classified ads in the magazines, checking bulletin boards in marinas and yacht clubs or by conducting searches on the Internet. You can also walk the wharves and dry-storage lots to see sailboats with "For Sale" signs hanging from their bow pulpits. Any of these sources is a good way to begin looking for the type of sailboat you want and can afford.

### Internet

Within a few short years, the Internet has changed the way we communicate, the way we gather information and the way we shop. And it's changed the way we look at boats. The Internet is a convenient tool and a data mine of immense proportions that can help your search for your trailerable sailboat, but there are pratfalls that must be avoided, unless you think that learning the hard way is the right way.

- Find the search engine that returns the best results for the boat(s) you are considering. Use a very simple benchmark search on several sites and compare the number of returns. Root out the sites with low returns. Either they have poor search technology or spotty listings.
- Note that many listings surface on multiple sites, just like they can be seen in different brokerage ads or classified print ads.
- Trolling eBay or other non-boating sites is not a good idea, because listings there often are last-ditch efforts to peddle something that no broker or seasoned buyer would touch.
- Distinguish between broker-driven sites such as www.yachtworld.com that list used boats like a central agency and rout your inquiry to the listing agent, and sites that include owners' listings, such as www.boats.com that facilitate direct contact.
- During your preliminary search, access the Web's incredible wealth of insider information for any given make and model. Enthusiastic owners are more likely to give you the lowdown than manufacturers or dealers, who have commercial interests. Register as a guest and join the discussion forums, ask questions and browse the FAQ libraries.
- To find owners' or class associations, visit the manufac-

turer's home page or www.boatowner.org, which lists
more than 100 owner-operated Web sites. Also check the
source listing at the end of this chapter. Aside from tech-
nical discussions, performance tips, line drawings, maintenance logs, recall and source information for spare
parts, these sites also help you gauge the "class culture"
and the level of involvement owners have with their boats.
A well-organized and updated site indicates an active and
thriving group, which will most likely be glad to help
potential newcomers.

- Look at boats in other areas to get a better feeling for asking prices and equipment, but don't assume anything. A
freshwater boat may look good online but it could be a
beaten-up charter boat, while the same model in New England
might have spent half its life in winter storage.

- Good sites provide access to independent boat reviews and
offer quotes for financing, surveyors, insurance and shipping. To get a loan quote online, be prepared to furnish some
sensitive info to third parties, such as mortgage, credit-card
payments, annual income, alimony, child support, etc.

Despite all these possibilities, there are limitations to what you
should expect from technology. Because the Web is egalitarian,
your research will not result in competitive advantage. Some sites
suggest that selling or buying directly saves money, because there's
no middleman and commission to pay. That could be true for very
small and simple boats such as dinghies or runabouts, but in most
cases the purchase of a cruising boat—even a trailerable one—tends
to be a complex, time-consuming process and mistakes can be expensive and painful. In that case, a licensed broker might still be
your best bet so you get what you want at the price you are willing
to pay. Bonded and licensed brokers want your money for the right
to represent you and a chance to absolve you from the chores, er-
rands and the pitfalls of potential fraud. See the end of this chapter
for a listing of sites to start your Internet buying search.

### Why Sellers Sell

When you find the boat of your dreams, it is useful to know why the person wants to sell. Usually people who sell their boats do it because they are no longer in tune with the sport and/or their boat. Too much work, too little time, a wife that has lost interest or kids who like horses better than boats: the reasons are endless. Because owners who want to get out of sailing, want to get out fairly quickly, there is a potential for a deal. This is especially true at the end of the boating season, when they want to unload the vessel so they won't get stuck with haul-out and winter storage costs etc. Others might want to trade up, like my friend who bought a 30-foot sailboat or get a newer version of the same model. If you can catch them after they have agreed to buy the bigger boat, and are "motivated" to sell their trailerable yacht, you can often get a pretty good deal. Then there are those poor souls who have liquidity problems, which could also result in good opportunities for buyers because the seller needs cold hard cash fast. But be prepared for anguished looks, misty eyes, and the wailing and gnashing of the seller's teeth, however, because most of these people really don't want to part with their beloved sailboats. A fourth group consists of sailors who have sailed their boats long and hard and are tired of repairing stuff that breaks. They have, as my son Jon says, "gotten all the goodie out of them." Stay away from them and you will avoid getting stuck with a lemon.

### Abandoned Sailboats

Some years ago I had a position with a college in the mountains of Southwest Virginia. The nature of my job required me to make frequent trips to Richmond. Since I have never enjoyed the sameness and boredom of driving on interstate highways, I would often travel the excellent backroads to Richmond. On one late summer trip I noticed a 22-foot trailerable sailboat parked in the driveway of a home just south of Richmond, and I made a mental note of it. A couple of months later I took the same route and the boat was still there, only this time the Virginia pines under which it had been parked had dropped their needles, and the boat was covered with brown straw. In the winter the snow had covered the pine needles and the trailer tires had gone flat. It was a shame. In the following spring I came that way again. The snow had melted, the pine straw was now limp and matted, and it looked like some sap was streaking down the hull. I had seen enough! I turned around, tracked down the owner and found out that even though he had not thought about it, he was interested in selling the boat at a reasonable price. I didn't buy the sailboat, but a friend of mine did. As bad as all of this sounds, such boats may represent the chance for you to make a terrific deal on a sailboat to which you can give a new birth, and enjoy sailing in real comfort. Admittedly, looking for a used sailboat in this way requires more time and effort, but it can pay you back through significant savings if you finally find the right boat.

## ➤ SURVEYING A USED BOAT ◄

Let's assume that you have looked at a number of used trailerables and located two in which you are really interested. Now it's time to pick up the telephone and arrange to take a careful look at them. Following is a list of the things I would want to examine. As you go through your inspection, keep a separate list of any problems you identify. If you can estimate the cost of repairing or replacing these items, it may influence the final price you are willing to pay for the boat.

As a second step, consider hiring a certified marine surveyor to go over your list of issues found and do a more rigorous check. You'll have to pay that person for that service, whether you buy or not, but if the boat has serious hidden issues, a few hundred dollars spent on a survey are much easier to absorb than purchasing a boat for several thousand that might require a big job by a professional boatyard in order to be seaworthy. Another simple piece of advice: Don't take a seller's survey for granted.

**Checklist for a DIY survey**

1. Hull and deck
2. Standing rigging
3. Running rigging
4. Keel and rudder
5. Sails and winches
6. Outboard motor and motor bracket
7. Electrical system
8. Hatches and lockers
9. Bilge
10. Berths, settees and cushions
11. Galley and head
12. Trailer
13. Sea trial

**Hull and Deck**

If the boat is in the water, you will need to put it on its trailer and haul it out. Take a long, careful look by standing at the bow and sighting down the hull. Look for waves, patches, discoloration, and blemishes. Waves may mean that the fiberglass for the hull was not laid up with a lot of care or in a shoddy mold, and this may reflect on the quality of construction of the whole boat. Run your hands down the side of the hull to determine if it feels smooth and even. If you see any areas of discoloration, the boat has probably been repaired in that area. That isn't necessarily bad, but you should get some explanation from the owner, and check the repair from inside the boat. While you are looking at the hull, notice any nicks and gouges. Don't expect used boats to be pristine, but be suspicious of large gouges that weren't fixed properly.

The deck inspection should focus on structural integrity and leaks first. Chances are that the gelcoat is weathered and oxidized, but that is just cosmetic. Look for cracks and soft spots as you walk around. Any noticeable weakness may indicate water seepage that has gotten into the laminate and core material, or that some very heavy object has crashed onto the deck creating hidden structural damage.

This is a critical test because structural repair work in these areas can be quite expensive. "Star cracks" in the gelcoat usually are the result of some localized stress, such as someone falling against a lifeline stanchion. It might be superficial, or it could be a sign of deeper trouble. Make sure you don't pass them up. Also pay attention to the seals of the port lights and hatches on the cabin top.

Next look at the integrity of the hull/deck joint. Ask the owner how it is built (bonded, bolted, screwed with self-tapping screws, etc.) and check for leakage and other signs of damage. Be especially thorough around the lifeline stanchions.

Check the deck hardware—winches, fairleads, cleats, etc.— and look on the inside to see how the fittings are backed. This too is a critical aspect because badly mounted deck hardware invites leaks, which weaken the laminate.

### Standing Rigging

If you can inspect the rig when it is on the ground you will be able to do a more thorough job. The mast on a trailerable boat is especially vulnerable in the parking lot when it is unstepped and tied to the deck for transportation. People back into obstacles, others can run into it and cause damage, therefore check the spars for bends, dents or other signs of misuse or neglect.

Make sure that all of the fittings on the mast are securely fastened and don't show signs of fatigue; they should all be stainless steel. Check the spreaders for bending or twisting, especially where they attach to the mast. If the overall appearance of the mast is good, take a look at the stays and shrouds. Check for broken strands and burrs. And pay close attention to the wire where it enters the turnbuckles and attaches to the mast because any sign of weakness and crevice corrosion here is bad news, and will more than likely mean replacing the whole thing.

If there are lights and a VHF antenna mounted at the mast top, see if they are properly installed and sealed. Also take a look at the wiring if it is kinked, stripped of its coating or otherwise compromised.

If everything looks acceptable on the ground, it's time to step the mast and secure it in place. Once the mast is up, make certain that it is properly aligned down the centerline of the boat and fore and aft, just in case it has a gentle bend that could not be detected on the ground. The boom should fit easily on the gooseneck and should work smoothly to both sides. Hold the boom level and check for any bends.

Finally, it is very important to take a look at the chainplates above and below deck to see if there is any sign of leakage, stress or corrosion and if the attachment to the hull (bolted and/or laminated) is intact and sound. Clearly, a failure in this area could cause the loss of the rig. Chain plates can be replaced, but it is neither a cheap nor a small job and needs to be done professionally.

### Running Rigging

The running rigging consists of the various sheets and halyards used to raise, lower, and control the sails. You should give them a good visual inspection and satisfy yourself that they are in good shape. Frayed or excessively worn running rigging is unsafe and will have to be replaced, and that can cost you a tidy sum.

### Keel and Rudder

If the boat has a fixed or swing keel check it for dents, nicks, and gouges. Again, don't expect it to look like it did when delivered from the factory—just make certain that it looks reasonably well and that there are no glaring cracks or fissures where it meets the hull. If the boat has a swing keel, you will want to do some additional checking when you do the sea trial.

Boats in our category most often have removable rudders, so pull it out of its mounting bracket and examine the pins that insert into the mounting bracket on the transom, making certain that they are solidly attached to the rudder. While you are at it, make sure the gudgeon on the transom is in good shape and firmly in place. Examine the rudder for straightness and previous damage. The leading and trailing edges of the rudder should be free of any deep gouges. If it is a kick-up rudder, make certain it can be brought to the up position fairly easily, and that the rudder blade can be fixed in its up and down positions and in between. Lastly, the tiller attachment to the rudder head should be firm without play, yet it should be possible to tilt it up with ease.

### Sails and Winches

Sails are the primary source of power for a sailboat and quite expensive to replace, so you need to make certain that they have received reasonable care and are in decent condition. If they were new, the seller would point that out immediately. Often, the sails are at the end of their useful life and your hope is that you might get one more season out of them. Assuming that you will be dealing with Dacron, not laminated high-tech racing sails, here are a few useful hints.

Spread them out on the ground to get an overall impression of their condition. Check the reinforced areas at the head, the tack, and the clew. Then work your way along the foot, the luff, and the leech to see if there are broken or flayed stitches and look closely at the stitching around the mainsail's batten pockets. Repeat on the other side. Discoloration and signs of chafe are part of the character of a used sail. Removing stains from sails is doing more harm than good because the aggressive solvents will damage cloth and seams.

Finally, check the boltrope or the slugs/battcars on the luff. Slugs should be intact, not broken and battcars with roller bearings need to slide easily on the track. If the boat has a roller furler for the jib, make sure the hardware is intact and that the drum rotates well in both directions when you pull the furling line. If everything looks pretty good so far, your next look at the sail wardrobe should be when it is hoisted, preferably for a sea trial. Do it yourself so you are familiar with the way the sails bend on and hoist. While you have them up, take another look at them to see if you missed anything during your ground inspection and trim them with all control lines. This will tell you if there is any life left. See if the mainsail's profile can be flattened by trimming the sheet, pulling the downhaul and the outhaul. And when you sail and a puff hits, see if the sail can hold its shape. If the cloth is worn and stretched, the camber of the sail will move aft as the wind pressure increases, which is a sign that the sail is in line for a demotion to a party sail or an awning for the patio at home.

Parallel to this test you ought to check the associated hardware. Do the cleats cleat? Do the blocks turn and do the winches grind properly? They should turn freely without much effort. If one doesn't, the bearings may be worn, indicating that they need to be serviced, rebuilt or replaced.

### Outboard Motor and Motor Bracket

With the boat on its trailer, the real test of the outboard motor will have to wait until you launch the boat. If the motor is not on the motor bracket, go ahead and put it on. This will allow you to get into the cockpit and see how well it works. You should be able to raise and lower the motor easily, and the bracket should lock in the up and down position for keeping the motor out of the water when under sail. The mounting block on the bracket should be in good shape (not cracked or broken), and the bracket should have no lateral movement, meaning it must be properly attached to the hull. Most likely, you can check the through-bolts and nuts from the inside, simply by peeking into the lazarette.

### Electrical System

When you buy a used trailerable sailboat it is quite probable that it will have some electrical and electronic equipment that comes with it, and often this equipment has been installed by the owner rather than by the factory or an electrician. So the first thing you should do is turning on the electrical panel. Then turn on the various systems: running lights, interior lights, VHF radio, etc. to see if all works properly. If that checks out, kill the power and turn your attention to the wiring. It is a common issue for surveyors to find shoddy, amateurish electrical wiring on used boats, which is expensive to fix and bring into compliance with the standards of the American Boat and Yacht Council (ABYC). Wires should be color-coded, labeled, bundled and routed so they are not subject to accidental snagging and/or separation. Properly installed electrical wiring is good insurance against battery drainage, inefficiency and, more importantly, fire.

### Hatches and Lockers

Make sure that the hatch covers are not warped or cracked, that they open and close easily, seal evenly, and that drains are clear. Take a look inside the lockers for cracks, fissures, and discoloration. Discoloration may indicate the presence of standing water, and you will want to look in the lockers again when the boat is in the water. If the boat has an anchor locker, you should make sure it's large enough to hold anchor and rode. Also check the inside of the locker to see if there are cracks that could have been caused by dropping a heavy anchor carelessly.

### Bilge

The bilge is the part of a boat located between the cabin sole and the bottom, where water collects. However, a lot of trailerable sailboats have no through-hull fittings, and you should check to see if the bilge is dry. If it isn't, ask the current owner where the water is coming from, if it is a leak in a water hose under the sink or if it might be from the engine cooling system if the boat has a built-in auxiliary engine. Also see if the bilge has an electrical and a manual back-up pump that are capable of extracting water quickly in a case of emergency.

### Berths, Settees, and Cushions

This is a quick and easy area to check. Lift up the settee and berth cushions and rub your hand along the top of the fiberglass seats and berths. They should be dry. Now look at the underside of the cushions for any water stains. If you see stains, or if the fiberglass tops of the berths and settees are wet, it could mean that water is seeping in at the hull-to-deck joint. If you do find dampness, you will need to ask the seller about it. Also make sure to lie down in the bunks to see if they are long and wide enough for you.

### Galley and Head

In the galley you need to make sure that the manual fresh-water pump works adequately. Second, check the fresh-water holding tank for leaks. If the boat has a galley that slides back and forth on runners, make certain the drain hose isn't bent, kinked, or leaking. If the boat has a propane stove, check the fuel line for chafe and possible leaks and the propane locker, which should be a vented compartment that's accessible from the cockpit. A defective propane system is a hazard with potentially catastrophic consequences, i.e. explosion. If there is an ice box, check the seals of the lid and if there are any cracks that could cause it to leak.

Most trailerable sailboats have been manufactured with a space to accommodate a porta-potti (chemical toilet). Some older trailerables were delivered with toilets that are no longer legal. Check that the toilet works, and that it is compliant with Coast Guard regulations for marine sanitation devices.

### Trailer

A lot of trailer sailors spend hour upon hour maintaining their boats and largely neglect their trailers. That's a shame, because without a reliable trailer a trailerable sailboat is just as immobile as a large deep-water cruiser. After you put the boat in the water, go back and take a close look at the trailer. It must be the right size for the boat you intend to buy. If you are not sure, contact the boat manufacturer to get a list of recommended trailers or check with the trailer company to see if the particular model was designed for the boat's weight. Next, you should examine the frame, the wheels, the electrical installation, and the boat supports.

Checking the frame, you are not going to be able to X-ray the welds for cracks, so about all you can do is making sure the welds are solid. Rust is a sign of corrosion, and it's ugly, and could be reason for alarm. Check any rust spots for their size and depth. Part of the frame is the winch post, which is more than a place for the winch that helps you retrieve the boat onto the trailer at the launch ramp. It also has a safety function that helps keep the boat on the trailer. Therefore it must be strong, properly bolted to the tongue and the bow roller should be above the eye.

If the trailer is equipped with a manual winch, check the cable for burrs, kinks and fraying. It should be long enough to allow retrieval of the boat on a shallow launch ramp and nicely align on the drum. On the winch itself check the ratchet mechanism and the attachment and length of the crank (longer is better). If the winch is good, it has two different gear ratios to multiply the grinders elbow grease.

The first thing about the wheels should be the condition of the tires. Do they have sufficient tread, do they have flat spots and is the rubber of the sidewalls cracked? If possible, take the wheels off and make sure the bearings are packed and the seals are in decent shape. A greasy film on the inside of the rim is a sign of a leaking bearing seal and a breakdown waiting to happen, because most likely seawater has seeped into the hub and started corrosion there. If the trailer has a torsion axle check the attachment bolts. Be wary of corrosion in this area. If the trailer is equipped with leaf springs, inspect springs, shackles, equalizers and pivot bolts.

Regarding the electrical installation, make sure the wires have not grown brittle from age. Follow them to their various destinations (lights, ground, etc.) and check for loose or corroded connections. Proper grounding requires the wire to go to the tow vehicle, not just the tow bar. If you see a section of bare wire without insulation, plan on replacing the entire section, or better, the entire wire harness. It won't cost a lot and it will save you trouble later. You also need to connect the trailer to the car's electrical system and make certain all of the lights work properly. (See Chapter 9, Trailer Tips for upgrade information).

Brakes are not a luxury for trailering a small cruising boat, they are a necessity and often mandated by state authorities. Depending on what kind of brakes the trailer has (hydraulic surge brakes or electrical brakes) your inspection might require a road trip to test their functionality. The least you can do is check for corrosion and if it is easy to move the brake coupler on trailers with surge brakes.

If the trailer has bunks for the boat to rest on, make sure they are intact and don't show edges or spotty carpeting. They should be through-bolted to their supports to prevent unintended loss and damage to the boat. Should the trailer have rollers, make certain that they roll freely, their support arms are straight and none is missing. They shouldn't have flat spots where they support the hull, because that will result in hull damage, especially when traveling on bumpy roads.

### Sea Trial

At last it's time for the fun part. When you board the boat be certain to ask the seller to tell you about any sailing characteristics that are unique to the boat. Knowing any characteristics peculiar to the boat may prevent some inadvertent damage, and it could save you some unnecessary embarrassment after you are under way. If you are not sure about your ability to judge the boat properly, ask a more experienced sailing friend to accompany you.

Before you hoist the sails, start the outboard motor. Check that it shifts smoothly from forward to neutral to reverse, and vice versa. Throttle the motor up and make certain it holds its rpms without tending the throttle, then throttle it back down. It is important to sail the boat like you envision sailing it when it is yours.

Also test the boat under engine alone to see how well it turns and responds to course changes. Back down and turn while going in reverse, and emulate maneuvering in a tightly packed marina.

While under way, check the handling on all points of sail, how the hull deals with waves and current. Observe how much water comes across the deck when the bow cuts through waves or ship wake. Listen for groans and creaks, check the bilges for water and watch the hull and the bulkheads for flexing. If the boat has a keel, open the floorboards and inspect the bolts while the boat sails and watch the chainplates when the boat sails to weather closehauled. These are areas of high stress and need to be sound.

See if the galley is functional enough to prepare coffee, a simple snack or sandwich while sailing. Can you access the cooler, can you boil water, can you reach the pickle jar? Do the same with the head. See if it is reasonable for an adult person to use it when the boat sails. Do you have to be Houdini to get to it and shed the foulies? Is there any privacy?

If the boat has a swing keel, you should check the cable as you winch it down. While you are sailing, keep your ears tuned to the possibility of hearing an occasional "thump, thump" sound in the vicinity of the swing keel. I hope you don't hear it, because it probably means that the through-bolt on which the swing keel pivots has wallowed out the keel. Such a condition is by no means terminal, but it needs to be addressed.

After you have been sailing for a while, recheck the inside of the lockers that showed discoloration during your earlier examination. If they are still dry, rainwater might have been the culprit.

Lastly, spend some "downtime" on the boat. If it is possible to drop the anchor, do so. It will show you the condition of the ground tackle and the rode and if it is easy to deploy and retrieve it. Go below and lie down. Listen to the sounds of the waves lapping up against the hull. Do they produce disproportionate noise when they hit the hull? Believe it or not, the noise of innocent small ripples can drive you crazy when you are trying to fall asleep.

## ➤ SUMMARY ◄

At the end of a personal survey don't jump to conclusions. Let the impressions that boat and previous owner have made settle in. Take a day or two to contemplate the good, the bad and the ugly. Have a professional marine surveyor check out the vessel and compare notes, or even better, hand him your notes about concerns you have found during your walk-through and sea trial, and accompany him when he does his inspection.

If you have absolutely fallen in love with the boat and want to own it, don't get carried away and pay the asking price. Listen closely to what the surveyor says or consult your own list of the problems you identified and get a rough estimate what it would cost to fix them. At a minimum you should adjust your offer to cover expected replacement expenses suggested by the problem list. As mentioned earlier, the Internet is a very good tool for comparison-shopping for boats of the same make and model year, so you know the range of asking prices.

If, on the other hand, the boat doesn't seem quite right for you, don't despair. Remember that there are lots of used trailerable sailboats on the market. You will have spent time and money to find out what you don't want and that is a valuable step on the learning curve. If you really want a pocket cruiser on a trailer, you will not rest until you have found it. Take my word for it.

## ➤ INFORMATION ONLINE ◄

The following listing of Web sites was compiled to help prospective and existing small-boat sailors with research of a spectrum of topics that include proper sail trim, suggestions for restorations and upgrades, prices and information about boating organizations and services that might be helpful for getting your first, next, or ultimate trailerable sailboat. Although all listings were checked for validity and accuracy at the time of this writing, the dynamic nature of the Internet makes it virtually impossible to compile URLs and call such a list complete and cast in stone. While some sites may change or go offline, most of them belong to large organizations that promise continuity and, more importantly, regular maintenance and updates to their online presence.

### Small-boat Web Sites

Not all small-boat cruisers are evangelists, but as a group they are very proud and outspoken about their favorite pastime, a trait that novices and seasoned boaters alike can use to their advantage to get up to speed on practically any topic. And that is not necessarily limited to sailing boats. If you have specific questions join their discussion forums or contact the sites' administrators for further information. They will be glad to help.

    www.boat-links.com
    www.boatowner.org
    www.sailboatowners.com
    www.trailersailor.com
    www.smallcraftadvisor.com

### Class Web Sites

The listings cover the boats discussed in this book. The sites can be affiliated with the respective manufacturers or run by an independent organization

    www.catalinaowners.com
    www.capri22.net
    www.catalina22.org
    www.com-pacowners.com/
    www.etapowners.org.uk/
    www.huntermarine.com/Owners/ClubsHSAs.html
    www.macgregor26x.com/
    www.macgregorowners.com/
    www.rhodes22.org
    www.santana22.com/

**Buyer's Resources**

## Suggested Web sites for buying new or pre-owned boats

> www.boats.com
> www.boattraderonline.com
> www.boatsville.com
> www.boatxchange.net
> www.boat-world.com
> www.everythingboats.com
> www.newboats.com
> www.usedboats.com
> www.yachtworld.com

**Important Boating Organizations**

It is not just what you know, but when you know it. Regardless where you are in your quest for a sailboat, countless organizations offer a wealth of information for existing or prospective owners that can be accessed instantly. A short sampling:

National Marine Manufacturers Association    www.nmma.org

Association of Certified Marine Surveyors    www.acms-usa.com

Society of Accredited Marine Surveyors    www.marinesurvey.org

U.S. Surveyors Association    www.navsurvey.com

National Marine Bankers Association    www.marinebankers.org

US Sailing    www.ussailing.org

Boat US    www.boatus.com

Yacht Brokers Association of America    www.ybaa.com

Coast Guard office of Boating Safety    www.uscgboating.org

Coast Guard Auxiliary    www.nws.cgaux.org

# 9
# *TRAILER TIPS*

## ➤ INTRODUCTION ≺

When hitched to the tow vehicle, your trailer is the one thing that gives you the freedom to "sail" down the highway to new lakes, rivers, and bays; it is also your personal ticket to unexplored coves, interesting anchorages, and new friends. But life on the road with a boat in tow is different from driving "unattached," so it makes good sense to go over a few parts of equipment you will need (or want to have) to make this part of the journey as smooth as a sail in a pleasant breeze at the end of a warm day. First order of business is getting there safely, preferably having car, trailer and boat arriving at your destination at the same time and in perfect condition.

### Legalities

But before you can launch you have to get to the ramp with a legal rig. Some states and municipalities may require special permits and licenses based on the size and weight of the trailer and if it is wider than eight feet. Inquire at the local motor vehicle administration to find out what requirements affect you. A good place to start is the National Highway Traffic Safety Administration (NHTSA) and their Web site at www.nhtsa.dot.gov.

### Floating Off

So you arrived at your destination in style and in one piece, beating the crowd to the launch ramp. Now the trailer becomes the center of attention. Will it aid or hinder ramp launching, especially if you have a boat with a fin keel? In order to push the trailer back far enough so the boat can float off, you might have to use a tongue extension and a ladder to get from the ramp to the winch post to untie the boat and take the painter to guide it over to the dock. It sounds like a complicated maneuver, but a trailer that's

Note the extended tongue, which makes it easier to ramp launch this fixed-keel cruiser.

short of key equipment often stands in the way of getting a trailer-able sailboat with a fixed keel far enough down the launch ramp.

To prevent such surprises, consider a so-called float-off trailer with keel guides, a winch, an extension bar and a swivel wheel at the front-end of the tongue. You may start your own research at one of the larger trailer manufacturers such as Triad (www.triadtrailers.com), Loadmaster (www.loadmastertrailerco.com), Pacific Trailers (www.pacifictrailers.com) who provide advice and a quote in case you are looking to replace/upgrade the wheels. Most likely they will have the construction drawings for the popular trailerboat models on file.

## ➤ GENERAL TRAILER ADVICE ≺

- Trailer tires must be properly inflated to reduce the risk of a flat. Driving with under-inflated tires is a common reason for trouble. Bring a spare wheel, not just a tire and inflate it with the proper air pressure before you leave. It will save you a lot of trouble.
- Wheel hubs and axles must be properly lubricated. Immersing hot hubs in cold water cools down the metal and produces a vacuum inside the hub, which sucks in water, which starts the degradation of the grease. One way to avoid that is putting on bearing protectors (bearing buddies). To make sure inner and outer bearings are properly lubricated, conduct a thorough annual check by removing all bearings, cleaning and repacking them.
- Tongue weight is a necessary evil for the proper handling of the entire rig. For a total trailer weight that's less than 1,500 lbs, calculate approximately 5 percent of tongue weight and 7 percent for trailers above 1,500 lbs gross. While that might seem hard on your hitch, it helps reduce trailer sway.
- Trailer lights have a life and a character of their own. Even frequent checking can't seem to help. For example: Who has never reversed a bayonet lamp in its sockets, and wondered why the bright and dim filaments come on at the wrong time? Insert the bulb guides in their proper slots and pack a kit of spares. You'll need it. Trailer wiring can be a plague too, but done right it should not interfere with your enjoyment of a road trip. See below for more on that topic.
- Never rely on the trailer winch strap or cable to secure the bow of your boat during trailer operation. Instead use a dedicated strap or line of appropriate strength to keep your boat on the trailer.
- If you use a transportation cover, tie it down. Flapping

covers reduce visibility even when they stay attached to boat or trailer and are a major hazard for others when they get carried away. They also have a habit of attracting the scrutiny of the Highway Patrol.

### Trailer Winches

Manual or electrical trailer winches are key instruments that help launching and retrieving your boat at the launch ramp. Unless you have an extension bar for the trailer tongue, the trailer sometimes can't be backed down in the water far enough for the boat to float on, so it has to be dragged up onto the bunks. This is an act that battles gravity and friction, which comes off a lot easier with some mechanical advantage. Trailer winches are mounted on the winch post far forward on the trailer tongue. Their spools hold up to 50 feet of cable, strap or nylon line, which is clipped to your boat's bow eye.

While there are terrific electrical models with capacities of up to 10,000 pounds, good mechanical winches with two gears (5:1 and 12:1) suffice for small trailerable sailboats with less than 3,000 pounds of weight. Use a winch that is rated for half the combined weight of your boat, fuel and gear. If your boat uses water ballast, you have to account for that too, since it will only drain when the boat is on the trailer.

Be careful to engage the ratchet when the cable comes under load and brace your feet. Launch ramps are often slippery and a fall can cause injury and damage to the boat. If the cable shows signs of wear, replace it immediately. Periodically lubricating the cable to reduce friction will extend its useful life. Alternatively, use a strong nylon rope or strap. Because winch cables or straps are not meant to secure the boat for transport, disconnect them and use a dedicated tie-down.

### Tie-downs

Securing the boat properly for the trip is a vital aspect for your own safety and that of others on the road. A good tie-down system has straps, hooks, ratchets and buckles that make securing your boat to the trailer a breeze compared to fiddling with ropes that are either slack or tight as a piano wire. A modest investment for tie-downs at the stern, at the gunwale and at the bow will give you peace of mind and protect your boat against sustaining and doing damage while on the road.

- Use ratchet straps to secure the stern and prevent the boat from bouncing or jumping off the trailer. They are easy to tighten and loosen, they spread loads over a wider area and they won't slide or roll like rope tends to do.
- Measure the distance between the attachment points on boat and trailer so you get the right length. If you sail in saltwater venues, consider tie-downs with stainless-steel hardware.
- If you're using a custom trailer for your boat, attachment points on the boat and the trailer should match. Otherwise, use strong eyes and cleats on the boat and run the tie-downs to the closest point on the trailer frame. You can add attachment points to the trailer frame with U-bolts or brackets.
- Avoid sharp edges and other chafe-points or pad the strap where necessary for protection. The wind forces that work on your boat while driving can destroy a compromised tie down, and nothing good can come from that.
- Throwing kit under the cover inside the cockpit or into the cabin and forgetting about it invites trouble because unsecured items such as tool boxes, spars, boat hooks etc. can damage the inside of your boat during a hard stop or in fast corners.
- To keep tie-down hooks in place use S-hook keepers that

prevent them from sliding out of their attachment eye while you put on tension. The same is true for the trailer's safety chain hooks, which can bounce out of their attachment points on the hitch if left unsecured.

### Trailer Lights and Wiring

A functioning set of trailer lights is not just a legal requirement, but also prevents others from running into your trailer and damage your boat, which is enough reason to spend a few moments on this topic.

You will need a wiring harness for the trailer's lights, a connecting plug that links it to the towing vehicle's lighting circuitry, and assorted lights around the perimeter. Most often trailers have multifunction lights that combine several lights in one fixture, which makes mounting and wiring easier.

The law requires that trailers that are less than 80" wide have taillights, stop lights, turn signals, side marker lights and side and rear reflectors on each side. You also need a light for the license plate and on trailers over certain lengths, marker lights and reflectors are necessary on each side. Trailers wider than 80" need to have three red identification lights facing rear and clearance lights on the fenders.

Corrosion, dirt, grime, vibration and occasional unintended contact with a hard obstacle are just a few enemies of working trailerlights. Thermal shock caused by immersion of hot lights in cold water is the death of filaments in old-fashioned incandescent bulbs and their plastic lenses. Voltage drop that is caused by high current draw from the lights on the trailer and the towing vehicle can be another source of headache.

If you immerse your trailer during launch, you need lights that are sealed permanently, have rubber gaskets or can be removed before you back down into the water. You could also switch from incandescent to LED lights, which is an engineering marvel that has quickly found acceptance in the automotive industry. It's a bit pricier but has too many advantages to be ignored, including life expectancy (100,000 hours) that is a multiple of typical incandescent lights. There are no filaments that break and no bulb bases to short or corrode because LEDs are better suited for contact with water and dirt, with a permanent seal in a welded polycarbonate lens. There's no danger of thermal shock, because LEDs don't generate heat and their low power draw minimizes the chances for a voltage drop.

If you are unhappy with your wiring, stop patching and start replacing it with a new harness. It's cheaper and faster to do than constantly fiddling with an unreliable rig, plus it will be easier on your nerves. To run wires through the trailer frame, use the old wires as a messenger. Mind the color codes when you do that. White is the ground wire, which should connect to the vehicle ground and the trailer frame. Brown is for taillights and runs the red taillights and to the clearance lights. Green (like in starboard) is for the right turn signal, and the yellow is for the left one.

If your vehicle has amber turn signals, or separate turn signals and break lights, consider using a cheap five-to-four wire converter to align trailer and vehicle wires. Use flexible stranded wire, and secure exposed stretches of wire with ties. Insert rubber grommets to protect the wires where they enter and exit the trailer frame. To wire the towing vehicle, ditch the test lamp and the wire splices in favor of a T-connect or instead of your car's original light plug. Get into the habit of inspecting the wiring and the lights at regular intervals, not just when you are hitched up and ready to go. Have silicone grease handy to dab dust caps and connectors, just to be on the safe side.

### Trailer Brakes

Even though most modern trailerable sailboats in our size range are not especially heavy (as boats go), they are probably nearly as heavy as your towing vehicle, unless you drive a Hummer. Going downhill with such a load turns brake-less trailers into a formidable pushing force, which can dangerously overpower the towing vehicle's brakes. If that happens, you don't need a lot of imagination to know what's next. Besides, brakes are required by law for trailers above certain weights, but these limits differ from state to state, so check with your DMV first.

- Hydraulic surge brakes: They are the most common brakes on trailers for small sailboats. These brakes are activated by the momentum of the trailer that pushes against the car when the car slows down. The trailer's brake action is triggered by a lever-and piston mechanism in the trailer tongue that activates the brakes with the help of a hydraulic master cylinder. Because surge brakes are passive, there's a moment of delay when the trailer pushes the car, which results in a longer distance to stop.
- Electric trailer brakes are activated by the brake pedal of the car. When that pedal is pushed down it electrically activates the trailer's brake cylinder via the brake controller, so the trailer always brakes first. There is no push, which increases safety, especially downhill. But be aware that electric brakes might not be offered for float-off trailers.
- Discs or drums: Like other vehicles, trailers can be fitted with either disc or drum brakes. The former are more efficient for heavy loads, but also more complex and expensive. Properly sized drum brakes should suffice for the kind of trailerable sailboats we are discussing in this book. Drum brakes have a return spring that functions both in forward and reverse. Disc brakes, as good as they are, are disengaged for backing up by a reverse lock-out solenoid switch, which leaves the trailer without braking power when you back down a launch ramp.
- Upgrading: If you have the least bit of doubt that your trailer needs better brakes, consider spending the money on the upgrade from drum to disc brakes. It's an investment in safety, just like emergency flares on your boat.

Most boaters probably will consult a professional for this job.

- Maintenance: Always rinse the brake system and the entire trailer with fresh water after ramp launching. To prevent salt build-up and corrosion on trailer brakes you could also try a salt removing spray such as it is used for flushing outboard engines. Lubricate caliper pins and moving parts, check fluid levels and monitor the wear of pads and shoes. If you use a trailer with electric brakes check the connection between vehicle and trailer.

### Safety Checklist

Now it's time to hit the road, but before you do, make it a habit to go through a short checklist even if the trip is only across town. It is much better to detect a possible problem before you have packed the cooler, the kids and the family dog for a fun weekend on the water than having to spend your hard-earned leisure time in a repair shop, or worse, sorting out insurance procedures after an accident. Here is what the National Highway Traffic Safety Administration recommends in one of their brochures about safe trailer operation:

- Check and correct tire pressure on the tow vehicle and trailer.
- Make sure the wheel lug nuts/bolts on the tow vehicle and trailer are tightened to the correct torque.
- Be sure the hitch, coupler, draw bar, and other equipment that connect the trailer and the tow vehicle are properly secured and adjusted.
- Check that the wiring is properly connected—not touching the road, but loose enough to make turns without disconnecting or damaging the wires. Make sure all running lights, brake lights, turn signals, and hazard lights are working.
- Verify that the brakes on the tow vehicle and trailer are

operating correctly. Check that all items are securely fastened
on and in the trailer.

- Be sure the trailer jack, tongue support, and any attached
  stabilizers are raised and locked in place.
- Check load distribution to make sure the tow vehicle and
  trailer are properly balanced front to back and side to side.
- Check side- and rear-view mirrors to make sure you have
  good visibility.
- Check routes and restrictions on bridges and tunnels.
- Make sure you have wheel chocks and jack stands.
- And above all, make sure the trailer's safety chain is
  crossed under the hitch, properly connected and secured to
  the tow vehicle.

One of the real joys of trailering your sailboat down the highway
is to see the folks in the passing cars ogle and drool with envy as
they watch you from their cars. Have fun and be safe.

# Epilogue

The following account is excerpted from a story published by *Die Yacht* in 2004. It describes the outer edge of possibilities for small boats and should not be construed as an endorsement. DL.

After I had finished work on the manuscript of *Sailing Big on a Small Sailboat*, I wondered what exactly made it so enjoyable. Surely it must have been the stroll down memory lane, the simple romance of youth, the carefree days of messing about in small boats. That's all we had and that's all we needed. Who was to tell us otherwise? But somehow, that didn't quite explain the matter. Then one day while on assignment in Europe, I heard an outlandish tale about a German sailing family, but to me it made complete sense.

In the summer of 2000, Hans and Carola Habeck and their then three-year-old son Andreas set sail on WAL, their brand-new Etap 21i in Colijnsplaat, Holland. It was a stock boat designed for inshore or lake sailing and was upgraded only with minimal additions for family cruising. It was all they could afford. With a few years of local sailing experience in the coastal waters of Northern Germany they weren't exactly blue-water veterans, but they were curious and adventurous. Their plan was to see how far they could get. After three years and nearly 30,000 miles they had their answer: once around. To someone like me, who remembers the small-boat heroes like Blondie Hasler, Robin Knox Johnston, or the early exploits of Francis Chichester, this adventure of the Habeck family has a nostalgic quality: Size wouldn't, couldn't matter. If it had, they'd be still sitting at the dock. One of my sailing friends called this endeavor "camping around the world." I call it "sailing far on a small sailboat" and enjoy a modicum of satisfaction that the Habecks put to good use several ideas that were discussed in this book.

Audacious or irresponsible, Hans and Carola Habeck were called all this and perhaps worse. But that shouldn't ruin their remarkable accomplishment that was based on spirit, discipline, luck and ability and the capacities of a small trailerable sailboat. WAL had no fridge, no radar, no hot water, no shower, no stereo system, no computer, not even a cabin table. "We didn't miss any of it," Hans told *Die Yacht*. Life was spartan and the confines were narrow, especially when it blew hard and everybody had to stay below deck. The galley consisted of a single-burner alcohol stove and one deep pot for cooking rice, noodles, veggies and warming up canned food. They had 50 gallons of fresh water stowed under the floorboards, which was enough for an entire month at sea, provided all three did not use more than 1.3 gallons a day. The mattresses were replaced by mats, which weren't susceptible to mold and could be rolled up if necessary. Because they believed the manufacturer's claim that an Etap is unsinkable, they saw no need for a bulky life raft and brought a small inflatable tender instead. The sails were set up for efficiency in the trades: Both jibs could be poled out and furled at a moment's notice without sending someone forward. The furling line, like all other sail controls, was led aft on the cabin top, so all adjustments could be made from the companionway while the trusted wind vane held the boat on course. The key to survival was resourcefulness, patience and defensive sailing. The Habecks chose the barefoot route along the trade wind belt and waited for suitable weather windows for long ocean passages. Except for the calmest of days, they sailed with lifebelts clipped on.

Their journey took them from the Netherlands past the Cape Verde Islands, across to St. Lucia, then through the Panama Canal to the Galápagos Islands and on to the Marquesas and Australia. After a seven-month stopover during which the boat was thoroughly checked and serviced, they carried on along the Great Barrier Reef and across the Indian Ocean to the Maldives. The last part through the Red Sea and the Suez Canal proved to be the toughest because of difficult weather and the fact that they found themselves between the fronts of the Iraq War that just had broken out. But WAL and her intrepid crew weathered it all and slipped into the Med to close the loop with a trip through the Canal du Midi into the Bay of Biscay and then on to the Netherlands, where they had slipped WAL's cables three years earlier.

Developing and executing a conservative game plan combined with sound practices of seamanship benefited the Habecks tremendously. First in the Atlantic, when they had to run before a storm under bare poles, dragging heavy lines to stay on course. Then from Panama to the Galápagos, when they took it on the nose for 10 days straight. Going 800 miles to weather takes sea room and a good deal of zen on any boat. Zen also helped them cope with a prolonged calm in the Indian Ocean, which tested their patience and ability to conserve water and food. And what about the child? Son Andreas, they say, loved every minute of it. Aside from getting the adventure of a lifetime, he enjoyed standing headroom in the entire cabin and pot-peeking privileges in the dwarfish galley. When his parents sailed the boat, he retired to his bunk playing with hand puppets or Legos. During stopovers he made a ton of new friends and learned to speak English.

But all this bravado should not disguise that WAL sailed under a lucky star, being spared major equipment trouble. During the Pacific crossing the boat collided with a sea turtle, about 380 miles out of Nuku-Hiva and lost the lower half of the starboard rudder. But an Etap 21i has a twin rudder system, so the defect was less dramatic than it would have been otherwise. Eventually, a replacement was jury-rigged and the family safely made port after a 3,124-mile crossing. During a 7-month stopover in Australia, Hans reinforced the attachment of the main bulkhead to the coachroof with stainless-steel bolts. Toward the end of the voyage they traded the minuscule 3.5-hp outboard for a 15-hp. model because they were running out of time and needed additional power to brave the headwinds in the Red Sea.

Afterwards the family settled in Germany, where Andreas attends school and where they are plotting their next adventure. They want a bigger yacht, but money matters. "Actually that's nonsense," Hans told *Die Yacht*. "After all, our boat is absolutely sufficient." That statement, I thought, is indicative of a true small-boat sailor: Go simple, go small, and don't worry. It'll be great.

# Notes and Credits

## Quotes

Reprinted by permission.

Leckey, Hugo, *Floating*. New York: W.W. Norton & Company, Inc. 1982

Maloney, E.S., *Chapman Piloting*. New York: Hearst Marine Books, 1989

Nicolson, Ian, *Comfort in the Cruising Yacht*. Dobbs Ferry, NY: Sheridan House Inc. 1987

Griffiths, Maurice, *Round the Cabin Table*. Dobbs Ferry, NY: Sheridan House Inc. 1985

Meisel, Tony, *Nautical Emergencies*. New York: W.W. Norton & Company, Inc. 1984

Davison, Anne, *My Ship Is So Small*. Leatherhead, Surrey: Ashford, Buchan & Enright, 1992

Graham, R.D., *Rough Passage*. US: Sheridan House Inc/UK: Seafarer Books, 2005

Payson, Herb, *Blown Away*. Dobbs Ferry, NY: Sheridan House Inc. 1995

Excerpt from *Die Yacht*.

## Illustrations

Photos:

| | |
|---|---|
| pages 11, 47, 48, 49 | Courtesy of Mac Gregor Yacht Corporation |
| pages 25, 27, 29, 30 | Courtesy of Catalina Yachts |
| pages 34, 35 | Courtesy of Com-Pac Yachts |
| pages 39, 40, 87 | Courtesy of Etap Marine LLC |
| pages 43, 44, 109 | Courtesy of Forest Johnson/Hunter Marine |
| pages 52, 53, 54, 99 | Courtesy of *Practical Sailor* Magazine |
| pages 56, 57 | Courtesy of W.D. Schock Corp. |
| page 222 | Courtesy of Triad Trailers |

| | |
|---|---|
| Figures: | 1-1 courtesy of Catalina Yachts |
| | 2-1, 2-2, 2-3, 2-4, 3-1, 3-2 by Donnie Cobb |

# Index